TAKE GOD'S HAND

Hope and Help for Rebuilding Your Family after Divorce

AIMEE CLAIRE COOKS

ISBN 979-8-89112-191-1 (Paperback)
ISBN 979-8-89112-192-8 (Digital)

Covenant Books
11661 Hwy 707
Murrells Inlet, SC 29576
www.covenantbooks.com

To my brave sons who faced their situation with
tenacity and used their circumstances to grow.
To my beautiful girl who was the most perfect surprise
addition to our family through adoption.
To my stepchildren who have their own stories.

Children are a gift from the Lord;
they are a reward from Him.

—Psalm 127:3 NLT

Contents

Introduction..vii
How to Read This Book..ix
CH 1 Getting to Know Your Guide 1
     Derailed by Divorce 1
     The Reality of Divorce 3
     Grief..5
     Moving from Human Rejection to God's Acceptance..........7
     God as Our Constant..9
CH 2 Trust Your Guide..15
     Prayer Is Talking to God..................................15
     Prayer Journaling..17
     God's Word: The Map for Our Journey..............19
     Our Minds..24
     Jonathans, Purahs, and Barnabases 25
     Counselors..28
     God Is Our Provider..29
     The Beautiful God Planned Life........................30
CH 3 Hidden Traps 34
     Unforgiveness..35
     Whitewashed Walls 36
     Anger and Revenge..39
     Power of Spoken Words....................................41
     Older Brother Syndrome..................................42
     Lawyers and Courts..45
     Comments That Cut..47
     Relationship Rescue...*Not!* 51
     Missing the Blessings..53

CH 4 Your Child's Story 56
      My Son's Stories 58
      What Your Children Need to Know about Divorce..........60
      God's Priority of Children 62
      God Cares and Has a Plan for Their Lives 66
CH 5 Single Parenting 71
      Changing Parental Roles 71
      Raising Men and Women of Character..........................73
      Power of Prevention 79
      Parenting Guidelines 83
      Power of Routines and the Power of Flexibility..............88
      Teaching Safety 89
      Asking for Forgiveness and Accountability 90
      Children's Activities 92
CH 6 Rebuilding Your Family..96
      Peaceful Abode 99
      A Word on Holidays 100
      Family Night 102
      Church..104
      Giving to Others 105
      Vacations..107
CH 7 Prayer: Your Most Powerful Tool 112
      Inner Strength..114
      Outward Protection..116
      Spiritual Growth 118
      Prayer for their Sibling Relationships..........................120
      Prayers for Friends 121
      Prayers for Their Future 121
      Praying for our Son's Futures......................................122
      Prayers for our Daughter's Future 125
Conclusion: Final Words of Hope 131
      Living in God's Strength...132
Acknowledgments 135
Connect 137
Appendix..139
References 141
Recommended Reading and Resources......................................145

INTRODUCTION

This was not my life plan. I was smart, patient, and wise. My marriage was thought out and going to last forever. We were going to do things "right." We went to premarital counseling with our pastor who had a great record of the couples he married staying married. I longed to be a stay-at-home mom. In fact, as a child, when people asked me what I wanted to be when I grew up, a "mom" was my answer. However, we could wait while I worked a few years until we had the "right" amount of money saved.

My career as a teacher of young children in an urban area led me to see so many children who either grew up in single-parent homes or chaotic blended families. These children carried backpacks with clothing instead of school supplies because they were going to be picked up by the other parent. Many times they had no idea who was picking them up. I always thought that this would not be my children; they would have better. They would not have the looks of confusion I saw on my students' faces. I would protect them from this.

My "right" life was going as planned. As soon as we tried, I became pregnant. My son was born, all natural, and he was the most beautiful, healthy boy. We were so proud, but as expected or maybe unexpected, babies shake up life a little. My then husband mourned how life had changed. One day, I sat in my son's bedroom, rocking him when he came and stood in the doorway. The only words I remember him saying are "I want to date other people." A relationship at work had become more, more than what we had. At that moment, I told him to leave.

After a short time, though, I determined I was not ready to give up this life I had worked so hard for. I knew marriage was hard work. We went to counseling. I am not sure if I exactly begged my husband, but I pleaded and brought out our premarital counseling papers and showed him what he had written. Did he still believe these things? I know I pleaded and begged God to save my marriage.

I was determined to show my husband that life with a baby can go on. I carried Garrett in a baby carrier so we could hike. We bought a bike trailer so we could still go on bike rides. These were all good things that I would do all over again, but also driven by the fact I wanted to convince my husband to love the life we had now. However, I was not secure enough in our marriage to relinquish my teaching contract and went back to work in a miraculous part-time position God provided. (My gracious God knew I would need this position later.)

After a time and counseling, I was ready to add to our family, but I needed to know my husband was ready too. We waited longer than what I thought was the "right" amount of time. Even at this point, I held tightly to my plan—I can see myself, symbolically speaking, with this tight grip on this piece of paper with my life plan on it—the wind and rain of life having tattered it; but I refused to release it. Almost three years later, we had another beautiful baby boy and named him Nathan.

He was six months old—a smiley, happy baby—and my husband left again following a family crisis. It was Mother's Day.

What do I notice about this season of my life? I was a Christian and I thought I loved God, but I did not completely trust Him with my life, only gave Him certain parts. I could handle the rest.

What now? I had a three-year-old and a nursing baby, no employment as I had quit my job to finally stay home (more on this later), and this time, my husband was not coming back. He, in fact, purchased a home not long after he left.

I had a choice: I could be angry with God (and some days I was) or I could put down my "rights," take His hand, and let Him lead me. I could confess my sin of doing life without including Him in every part. I am so glad I did because it has resulted in a sweet intimacy with my Jesus. This was not my life plan, but it was the God planned life for drawing me close to Him. I let go of the tattered piece of paper and took God's Hand.

"I know not the way God leads me, but well do I know my Guide" (Martin Luther).

How to Read This Book

The goal of this book is to bring you into a closer relationship with your Creator. Therefore, I encourage you to read this book with a Bible next to you. The goal is for you to be immersed in God's Word so He speaks life into your own unique story. My prayer is that God uses our story to bring life and hope to your story.

The end of each chapter has questions and options for you to begin to write and process your story. If this book does nothing else, I pray it makes you hungry for God's Word and to walk in a closer, intimate relationship with Him that you ever thought possible.

GETTING TO KNOW YOUR GUIDE

You're my cave to hide in, my cliff to climb,
Be my safe leader, be my true mountain guide.
Free me from hidden traps;
I want to hide in you, I've put my life in your hands.
You won't drop me, you'll never let me down.
Psalm 31:3–5 MSG

Derailed by Divorce

This book is about rebuilding your life and your children's life after divorce. If there is any chance, you could still work on your marriage, please take that chance. Even though my marriage did not ultimately work out, I do not regret any effort I made toward working on my marriage. If there is any kind of abuse in your marriage, emotional or physical, seek help. God does not desire for you or your children to tolerate abuse.

I feel like I have to begin by saying I am not advocating for divorce, but divorce is a reality in our society, even in the church. At times, I think the church is fearful of talking about divorce as not to seem condoning of it. Where does that leave the families who have been impacted by divorce who need hope and help? I remember being in a Bible study with an older woman, and when she talked of her divorce, it seemed like her pain was so new even after all those years. I wondered if the church had anything to do with the unhealed pain. I recall after my divorce another Christian telling me I could never get married again without being in sin. Fortunately, I also had Christians around me who supported me and gave grace. Unfortunately, there were few resources eighteen years ago for Christians who were in my same position.

What should be our view on divorce? Our view should be that of God's view. See Malachi 2:14–16. The beginning of verse 16 in the Message version uses this strong wording, "I hate divorce," says the God of Israel. God-of-the-Angel-Armies says, "I hate the violent dismembering of the 'one flesh' of marriage." Jesus reiterates this in the New Testament. See Mark 10:1–12 and Deuteronomy 24:1. The footnote regarding verse 5 in the NIV Study Bible states,

> Divorce was an accommodation to human weakness and used to bring order in a society that had disregarded God's will, but was not the standard God had originally intended, as vv. 6-9 clearly indicate. The purpose of Dt. 24:1 was not to make divorce acceptable, but to reduce the hardship of its consequences.

God absolutely hates sin and divorce, but God loves us. For the sole fact that there is sin in this world, there will be divorce until Jesus comes back. At the moment, you may feel "derailed." You thought you knew where your life and family were headed, and that is no longer the case. However you ended up in this situation you are in, this is where you are. I desire for you to know there is hope for your future and a new direction for your children and for your family.

God spoke this message to me through a photograph. When my husband left, we had a trip planned to California with family. We could not get a refund on tickets, so I went alone with the boys. My sister took a picture of us from a distance walking down the beach along the ocean. I was holding Garrett's hand and carrying Nate in a front baby carrier. I was unaware she took the picture until she gave it to me a few weeks later. For whatever reason, when she gave it to me, I knew. I knew that our path was going to be different, and I also had a God-given peace that I was not alone. The God who created the ocean and the God whose thoughts about me outnumbered the grains of sand was with me (see Psalms 139:17–18).

The God who created the ocean and the God whose thoughts about me outnumbered the grains of sand was with me.

The Reality of Divorce

I run to you, God; I run for dear life.
Don't let me down! Take me seriously this time!
Get down on my level and listen,
and please—no procrastination!
Psalm 31:1–2 MSG

When I was in a position where divorce was imminent, someone gave me a book called *The Good Divorce.* I am sorry, but having lived it, I do not think "good" and "divorce" should be included in the same title or sentence for that matter. Maybe there are better ways of doing divorce, but it is almost never good. Referring back again to Mark 10:5–9, the Message version says,

> Jesus said, "Moses wrote this command only as a concession to your hardhearted ways. In the original creation, God made male and female to be together. Because of this, a man leaves father and mother, and in marriage becomes one flesh with a woman-no longer two individuals, but forming a new unity. Because God created this organic union of the two sexes, no one should desecrate his art by cutting them apart."

Even the *American Heritage Dictionary* defines *divorce* as "a complete and radical severance of closely connected things." Severance is indefinitely going to cause damage; that damage is done to the souls of those involved. The solution to any damage of our souls is to do what Psalm 31 begins with "I run to you, God; I run for dear life. Don't let me down!" I continually marvel at how our Savior walked on this earth, felt what we feel, and therefore, is able to be with us in our pain like no one else.

I know I am writing to parents in many different circumstances. You may be divorced with shared custody or divorced with primary custody. There are endless arrangements of how children go back and forth between parents. Maybe you are able to work well with your ex-spouse for the welfare of your children. Maybe you are raising children alone now or maybe things change yearly. I hope that you will find a nugget in this book that brings you hope and comfort whatever the circumstances. Mostly, I pray you will find Jesus in your unique circumstances.

When my husband left, I had a three-year-old and a six-month-old. I had just quit my job when my second son was born. Their dad stayed in their lives, which I am truly grateful for. However, it became a high-conflict situation with communication only through an internet program and decisions eventually made through a court-ordered mediator. That said there are wounds left in my children's lives from the tension of having parents who were not only not together but could not even communicate. If you are able, consider coparenting classes with your ex-spouse. It was something I requested that my ex-husband was not up for. However, we were blessed to have a mediator for so many years who made decisions when conflict arose. Although not always in my favor, he did his best to be fair. I am thankful, but I am always amazed when I look back at how I survived those years of conflict. I could not have done it without Jesus.

Although my divorce, single parenting, years of court, and mediation were not easy, they were the circumstances that truly helped me to practice relying on God rather than my own strength.

Grief

I've cried my eyes out; I feel hollow inside.
My life leaks away, groan by groan;
My years fade out in sighs.
My troubles have worn me out,
Turned my bones to powder.
Psalm 31:9–10 MSG

No one had died, right? My boys still had their dad. So why did I feel like someone had died? Suppertime was the hardest. I would almost wait for my husband to come home so I could have some adult conversation after a day with my two young sons. My son would say his first word, and there was not a spouse to share it with. I would sometimes forget that my husband was not coming home or that I could not call him and share details of the day. I had to mourn all the lost dreams of what our family would have looked like—vacations, holidays, being a stay-at-home mom, etc.

The five stages of grief you may recognize yourself in are denial, anger, bargaining, depression, and acceptance. Be patient with yourself. I would feel like I was done with a stage, only to begin again and cycle through the stages. Sometimes it is a linear process, and sometimes you bounce around from one stage to another. Let your emotions have this time to grieve what was lost. It is part of the healing process.

I titled the day of my divorce the "funeral of my marriage." Even now as I write this, I remember the emotion as I sat on the stand in the courtroom. I stood in church and vowed to love this man for the rest of my life no matter what the circumstances. Now I sat in court, denouncing the very serious vows I had made before God.

Even years after the divorce, I would hear of someone else going through a divorce and have to cycle back through some stages of grief. Fifteen years later, when my current husband and I were adopting our daughter through the foster care system, I was back in the same courtrooms; and the emotions, tension, and uncertainty reemerged in my body. Becoming familiar with the grief stages is helpful so you can recognize which stage you are in. The work you do will carry over to how children process through their own grief.

Eventually, I was able to live in the acceptance stage most days. I would repeat to myself the second part of Job 1:21 (NASB): "The Lord gave and the Lord has taken away. Blessed be the name of the Lord." And may I do my best to be like Job.

"Despite all this, Job did not sin, nor did he blame God" (Job 1:22 NASB).

I did not repeat this as a victim or martyr. It was my way of accepting and recognizing God's sovereignty over my life.

The definition of *grief* from *vocabulary.com* is as follows:

> The word grief comes from the Latin word gravare, which means **to make heavy**. Gravare itself comes from the Latin word gravis, which means weighty. So think of grief as a heavy, oppressive sadness. We associate it most often with mourning a loved one's death, but it can follow any kind of loss.

The good news and hope for us is because Jesus accepted God's plan, we do not have to stay lost in grief or weighed down with grief. We bring our grief to Him and He will heal our souls. First Peter 2:24–25 (MSG) reads, "His wounds became your healing. You were lost sheep with no idea who you were or where you were going. Now you're named and kept for good by the Shepherd of your souls." Do you hear that? Jesus desires to be the Shepherd of your soul. Think about what a shepherd does for his sheep. He guides, protects, and attends to all their needs. This is what Jesus does for our souls.

Jesus desires to be the Shepherd of your soul.

Therefore, we look to our example of Jesus who knows how we feel because He has been there. Luke 22:44 (NASB) states, "And being in agony He was praying fervently; and His sweat became like drops of blood, falling down upon the ground." First, Jesus was able to verbalize his emotions. In Mark 14:34 (NASB), Jesus names the grief when he says to his disciples, "My soul is deeply grieved to the point of death; remain here and keep watch." Secondly, Jesus accepts God's will. Luke 22:42 (NASB) says, "He knelt down and began to pray, 'Father, if You are willing, remove this cup from Me, yet not My will, but Yours be done."

Being able to identify our emotions is a gift from God. The more you are able to recognize your emotions as Jesus did, the healthier you will be for your own sake and the sake of your children. Proverbs say the purposes or motives of a man's heart are deep waters, but a man of understanding draws them out (Proverbs 20:5). Even after nineteen years of being divorced, grief still comes back. I grieved that I could not share college plans with my son's dad. Every year, their birthdays were always a little bittersweet for me as I could not share them with a spouse. However, recognizing those feelings is powerful, and I am able to turn it over to God—the Shepherd of my soul.

Jesus calls for us to run to him with our burdens, with our grief, and in Him, we will find rest for our souls. "Come to me, all who are weary and burdened, and I will give you rest. Take My yoke upon you and learn from Me, for I am gentle and humble in heart, and you will find rest for your souls. For My yoke is easy and My burden is light" (Matthew 11:28–30 NASB).

Moving from Human Rejection to God's Acceptance

> Even my close friend in whom I trusted,
> Who ate my bread,
> Has lifted up his heel against me.
> Psalm 41:9 NASB

We find that Jesus not only faced grief but rejection as well. Looking at the gospel of Matthew 26:23 (MSG), Jesus says, "The one who hands me over is someone I eat with daily, one who passes me food at the table." Verses 47 through 49 continue with the story of Judas's betrayal:

> The words were barely out of his mouth when
> Judas (the one from the Twelve) showed up, and

with him a gang from the high priests and religious leaders brandishing swords and clubs. The betrayer had worked out a sign with them: "The one I kiss, that's the one—seize him." He went straight to Jesus, greeted him, "How are you, Rabbi?" and kissed him.

In Hebrew tradition, a kiss was a sign of loyalty. *The Moody Bible Commentary* states, "But the familiarity and (false) affection of the act made the betrayal that much more heinous."

Rejection is a part of life. However, when the one we unite our body and soul with rejects us, it is a deep wound. One verse that became precious to me when dealing with rejection was: "For my father and my mother have forsaken me, But the Lord will take me up" (Psalm 27:10 NASB).

I suggest putting your name right in the verse. I looked up this verse in different Bible versions. I would say, "For my husband has forsaken me but God took Aimee up, received Aimee, gathered Aimee up, took Aimee in." Jesus not only understands the pain of rejection, but He is there with open arms to accept us.

I also want to note that rejection can come in other ways in marriage. My experience is a spouse leaving physically, but there are other types of rejection. A spouse may choose alcohol or drug use over a marriage, and you may have made the hard decision to leave. You may have needed to leave due to physical, emotional, or verbal abuse. This is still a rejection that hits the core of our soul.

Jesus faced the ultimate rejection when He was on the cross and separated from His Father. In Matthew 27, verse 46, Jesus cries out, "My God, My God why have you forsaken me?" He faced rejection, so we could be accepted. He faced separation from God, so we never have to. When Jesus died, the veil of the temple was torn in two from top to bottom so we have direct access to God through Jesus. Jesus left the Holy Spirit with us. John 14:16 (NASB) reads, "I will ask the Father, and He will give you another Helper, so that He may be with you forever."

God as Our Constant

The Lord is the one who goes ahead of you;
He will be with you. He will not fail you or
forsake you. Do not fear or be dismayed.
Deuteronomy 31:8 NASB

This has always been my name, and
this is how I always will be known.
Exodus 3:15 MSG

When I planned my first wedding, I spent time planning the ceremony. This, to me, was more important than the celebration after. Years later, I looked back to see the pastor had begun the sermon with the scripture concerning God is always with us even to the end of the age. My earthly marriage covenant may be broken, but there is a relationship I entered into as a five-year-old girl with a tender heart that will never end. Earthly marriage covenants state until "death do us part," but not even death can separate us from the love of God. See Romans 8:38–39 (NASB): "For I am convinced that neither death, nor life, nor angels, nor principalities, nor things present, nor things to come, nor powers, nor height, nor depth, nor any other created thing will be able to separate us from the love of God that is in Christ Jesus our Lord."

Earthly marriage covenants state until "death do us part," but not even death can separate us from the love of God.

Heraclitus, the Greek philosopher, said, "Change is the only constant in life." This may be true, but I would like to counter that with the scripture from James 1:17 (NASB), "Every good thing given and every perfect gift is from above, coming down from the Father of lights, with whom there is no variation or shifting shadow."

If you are a Jesus follower, you do have a constant. People change; circumstances change, but our God stays the same. His love for us stays the same. He will always walk by our side.

God is always waiting for us to open the door and invite Him into our lives. Invite Him into our lives *and* let Him lead our lives which is something I needed to learn. In the next chapter, we will explore ways of how to let God hold your hand and be your guide.

Applications
Chapter 1: Know Your Guide

1. How do you view your divorce? How has it impacted your relationship with God?

2. What were your plans and dreams for your family?

3. This quote is from a fictional book, *Sensible Shoes*, but it resonates with truth.

    "Spiritual and emotional deaths are no less significant than the physical ones, but they can be harder to name."

    Name your dreams because you need to grieve each one. Processing grief releases us to enjoy new dreams and new visions for our family. One thing I had to grieve was not being able to have more children. I had wanted a large family. I had to grieve, not only not being a full-time, stay-at-home mom, but not having my children with me for periods of time.

    What dreams do you need to grieve?

4. What stages of grief have you passed through? Where do you seem to stay stuck?

    Journal about each stage.

    Grief stages:
    - Denial
    - Anger
    - Bargaining
    - Depression
    - Acceptance

Let Jesus sit with you in your grief. "Praise be to the Lord, to God our Savior, who daily bears our burdens" (Psalm 68:19 NIV).

5. Often, our view of God is tainted by our earthly relationships with others.
    Do you place any of those earthly qualities on God?
    Dwell on these truths about God.
    - God does not leave us (Deuteronomy 31:6; Isaiah 43:2).
    - God is faithful and keeps His promises (Psalm 145:13).
    - God loves us immensely with a never ending love (Psalm 100:5).
    - Nothing can separate us from God's love (Romans 8:31–39).
    - God loves us with a perfect love (1 John 4:16–21).

6. Add your own thoughts about God's truths here.

7. What verses speak to you the most? What other verses speak to you about how God views you?

8. What is the hardest part of your day? What can you do to take care of yourself and ease your heartache? (For me, the hardest part of the day was dinnertime when I expected my husband to walk through the door.)

Divorce can rob us of our confidence and self-esteem. We may need to take time to work on changing or reworking our belief system. I did this with a counselor a few years after my divorce.

We have had many words/labels spoken over us during our lives…by others and even by the words we apply to ourselves. For some reason, the negative words often stick with us, stick to us.

Applying God's Word to our lives is the way to overcome it. His Word is living, active, penetrating the soul and spirit, judging the heart and attitude.

Because of the gift of Jesus, and only because of Jesus, we are children of God with all the benefits of our heavenly Father's love for us. Add your names in the blanks. Because I think men and women process differently, I have asked my husband to make a chart that will speak more to the male perspective. That chart follows. (Both charts are also available as printables on aimeecooks.com under Resources.)

God declares in Christ _______ is	Scripture Reference	Verse (Insert your name in the blanks)
Loved	John 3:16 NASB 1995	For God so loved _______________________, that He gave His only begotten Son, that whoever believes in Him shall not perish, but have eternal life.
Valued	Psalm 27:10 NASB 1995	For my father and my mother have forsaken me, But the LORD will take up (or receive) _______________________.
A Conqueror	Romans 8:37 NASB 1995	But in all things _______________________ overwhelming conquerors through Him who loved her.
Beloved and Chosen	I Thessalonians 1:4 NASB	_______________________ — beloved by God His choice of you
His	Isaiah 43:1 NASB	Do not fear, for I have redeemed _______________________ I have called her by name She is Mine.
Precious	Isaiah 43:4 NASB	_______________________ is precious in My sight She is honored and I love her.
Hephzibah	Isaiah 62:4 NASB	_______________________ will be called "My delight is in her."

A Crown of Beauty (of high merit and honor) and a Royal Diadem	Isaiah 62:3 NASB MSG	____________________ will be called a crown of beauty in the hand of the Lord (or in the palm of God's hand) And a royal diadem in the hand of your God.
Belonging to Him	Isaiah 44:5 NASB	And another will write on His hand "belonging to the Lord."
Known to Him	John 10:27 NASB 1995	____________________ hears my voice and I know her.
Protected	John 10:28–29 NASB 1995	____________________ is protected from the Destroyer for good. No one can steal her out of my hand. The Father who put her under my care is so much greater than the Destroyer and Thief.
Child of God	1 John 3:1 NASB 1995	See how great a love the Father has bestowed on ____________________ that she would be called a child of God.
Supported	Romans 8:31–34 NASB	What then shall we say to these things? If God *is* for ____________________, who *is* against her? He who did not spare His own Son, but delivered Him over for. ____________________, how will He not also with Him freely give her all things? Who will bring charges against God's elect? God is the one who justifies; who is the one who condemns? Christ Jesus is He who died, but rather, was raised, who is at the right hand of God, who also intercedes for ____________________.
Remembered	Isaiah 49:16 NASB	Even these may forget, but I will not forget ____________________. Behold, I have inscribed her on the palms *of My hands*; Her walls are continually before Me.

A belief system chart from the male perspective and a thank-you to my husband, Ryan.

God declares in Christ _______ is:	Scripture Reference	Verse
Chosen	John 15:16 MSG	You didn't choose me, remember; I chose you, and put you in the world to bear fruit, fruit that won't spoil. As fruit bearers, whatever you ask the Father in relation to me, he gives you.
His Son and Heir	Galatians 4:7 ESV	Therefore you are no longer a slave, but a son; and if a son, then an heir through God.
Image Bearer	Romans 8:29 ESV	For those whom He foreknew, He also predestined to become conformed to the image of His Son.
Justified and Glorified	Romans 8:30 NIV	And those he predestined, he also called; those he called, he also justified; those he justified, he also glorified.
Redeemed	Job 33:28 NASB	He has redeemed my soul from going to the pit, And my life will see the light.
Useful	2 Timothy 1:7 NIV	For the Spirit God gave us does not make us timid, but gives us power, love and self-discipline.
Branch of the True Vine	John 15:5 NASB	I am the vine, you are the branches; the one who remains in Me, and I in him bears much fruit, for apart from Me you can do nothing.
Accepted	Romans 15:7 NIV	Accept one another, then, just as Christ accepted you, in order to bring praise to God.
New Creation	2 Corinthians 5:17 ESV	Therefore if anyone is in Christ, this person is a new creation; the old things passed away; behold, new things have come.

TRUST YOUR GUIDE

I want to hide in you.
I've put my life in your hands.
You won't drop me, You'll never let me down.
Psalm 31:3–5 MSG

Prayer Is Talking to God

The premise of prayer is that we are spoken to by God.
He calls us into being by his Word and leads us
into personal relationship by his Word.
What is the normal response of a person spoken
to? Is it not to reply? Prayer is the reply.
On Living Well by Eugene Peterson

This is not a time in life to make prayer complicated. Prayer, really, is just talking to God. He will listen. He has all the time in the world for you. I love the story of Jesus calling the children to sit on his lap. We are never too old for this story. Sit on Jesus's lap and tell him everything. He can handle all your emotions. Sometimes I feel like I have these boxes inside of my soul that I am hiding from God. I don't open them to Him. When I realize I am doing that, I almost laugh out loud to myself—or maybe I actually laugh out loud; I have been known to talk to myself or so my family tells me. Did I think I could really hide anything from Him? He already knew, but somehow, it lifts a huge burden for me to admit it and ask him to change me to be more like Him. Hide in Him, not from Him.

Hide in Him, not from Him.

There is not a concern in our life that is too small to tell Jesus. One thing I missed about marriage was being able to talk through things with another adult. The end of the day was the hardest time. I kept expecting my husband to walk through the door. To comfort that loneliness, I would turn on NPR (National Public Radio) just to have a voice. That was a temporary but useful tactic. However, God is the permanent solution for our loneliness. He truly cares about every detail of our lives and our children's lives.

I truly encourage you to find a place in your home where you daily meet with God. Find a time that works in your schedule. My morning prayer time has become a lifeline for me, even after all these years. When I wake up late or miss my prayer time, I feel like I forgot my morning cup of coffee. It focuses my mind for the day. No matter how small your home may be, have a dedicated prayer spot. My kitchen table was my original God and my meeting place. I kept a basket with my Bible and devotionals I could cart around so I was ready to go once I sat down. The kitchen table was my great-grandmother's table. It was pushed up against the wall in our small kitchen and pulled out when more than the three of us were there for dinner. That table had gone through a lot too. When I first received it, it was painted yellow hiding the real wood underneath.

One summer, I had stripped off the paint to reveal the wood grain. I stained it to show off the real wood grain. Is that not what God was doing with me too? Taking off that facade of serving Him but not truly trusting Him. Was not God making me a more real version of me, more of a representative of who I really was made in the image of God?

There will also be days when a formal meeting with God just does not happen. There were days I got up at 4:00 a.m. to do lesson plans and missed my prayer time. God is gracious and understands our unique circumstances. God hears and loves those prayers whispered throughout the day too when you don't have time for extended prayer. Psalm 31 says to talk to God all day—"hour by hour I place my life in Your hands." There are many helpful books on prayer, so I will not cover details here, but I will list my favorites in the appendix. It does help to have a routine or order to keep your mind focused. A simple order is to praise, thank, confess, and ask. Learn the names of God and praise God for who He is, thank God for what He has done (even if it is just for the strength to get out of bed that morning), confess sin so there is no blockage between you and God, and ask or let your requests be known to God.

It scares me to think of, if I had not met with these trials, would I be as close to Jesus as I am now? In that way, I am grateful for the circumstances He has used to grow me up. You may not be able to see or say that now, but know God is at work.

Eugene Peterson writes, "We commonly think of prayer as a court of last resort, what we do when we have exhausted our own resources and things still don't work. But prayer is not trying to get God to do what we can't do ourselves; it is getting in on what God is already doing."

Prayer Journaling

Cast all your anxiety on him because he cares for you.
1 Peter 5:7 NIV

Around this time in my life, I also started keeping prayer journals. I encourage you to dedicate a notebook to journaling your prayers. You do not have to be a writer and no one even has to be able to read it except you and God. Include all the good things God has done in your life and all the things you're grateful for (more on this later). Write down your concerns and prayers. Write down scriptures that have spoken to you that day. There are a few reasons I believe prayer journaling can be helpful in our walk with God.

First, it is a physical way of taking our thoughts and presenting them before God. I like the Message translation for Philippians 4:6–7.

Don't fret or worry. Instead of worrying, pray. Let petitions and praises shape your worries into prayers, letting God know your concerns. Before you know it, a sense of God's wholeness, everything coming together for good, will come and settle you down. It's wonderful what happens when Christ displaces worry at the center of your life.

Secondly, God continually told Israel to commemorate events of His works. In Joshua 4, God instructs Joshua to tell one man from each tribe to get a stone. The stone was to "serve as a sign among you" to remember how God had stopped the flow of the Jordan. The stones were meant to be a "memorial to the people of Israel forever." How quickly our human minds forget how God worked in the past in our lives. Our written words of how He has answered prayer in our lives become our "stones." I now have eighteen years of journals that I can look back on when I start to doubt how God has taken care of me, of my family, of all the situations we have faced in life. I recently read this in *Conversations: The Message with Its Translator* by Eugene Peterson:

> Forgetfulness is one of the great breaches in our relationship with God, for when we forget his saving ways, either in biblical history or in our personal history, the results are disastrous. Making memorials, whether they are stone monuments or journal entries, is the best way to keep from forgetting how good he has been to us.

Thirdly, writing down scriptures is a way to cement them in your head. Writing scripture prayers over you and your family is powerful. In those times, when you are rushed for time, open your notebook and pray out loud the scriptures God has given you. Finally, God and you are writing your story. Your story will not be like anyone else's story. Your journey will be uniquely used by God.

God's Word: The Map for Our Journey

But his delight is in the Law of the Lord,
And on His Law he meditates day and night.
He will be like a tree planted by streams of water,
Which yields its fruit in its season, And its leaf does not wither;
And in whatever he does, he prospers.
Psalm 1:2–3 NIV

Prayer and God's Word are so intertwined. They cannot be separated, although I have included them in different sections. Even when you read this book, read it with a Bible nearby. Look up the scriptures mentioned. God's Word truly is the only book you need. How do we get to know our guide? We study the map He left us. That map is His Word. It is a lamp to our feet and a light to our path.

This quote is from the German pastor Dietrich Bonhoeffer's book, *Life Together*:

> Often we are so burdened and overwhelmed with thoughts, images, and concerns that it may take a long time before God's Word has swept all else aside and come through. But it will surely come, just as surely as God Himself has come to men and will come again. This is the very reason why we begin our meditation with the prayer that God may send His Holy Spirit to us through His Word and reveal His Word to us and enlighten us.

Ask God to reveal His Word and then read it! The Bible provides us with everything we need during a time of trial. God will answer you and give you exactly what you need for the day. I will just touch on a few reasons to immerse yourself in God's Word.

During times of trial such as divorce, we need immense wisdom. Parenting is hard; parenting divorced is harder. The kind of wisdom we need is found in the Bible. "But if any of you lacks wisdom, let him ask of God, who gives to all generously and without reproach, and it will be given to him" (James 1:5 NASB). In the next chapter, "Hidden Traps," I will talk more about how we need God's wisdom because what seems right to a man is not always God's way (Proverbs 14:12).

The Bible shows us how much God thinks of us and loves us. He is looking upon you, upon your children with a face full of compassion. Take note of all the times in the gospels where Jesus looks at people and has compassion on them. Sometimes, it is worded as Jesus was moved with compassion. The word *move* in the *Merriam-Webster Dictionary* is defined as "to stir the emotions, feelings, or passions of." This shows it was a strong emotion, not just a fleeting passing one. Humans may have moments of compassion, but often, in a few minutes, we are on to the next thing. Not so with Jesus. You're always on His mind. Psalm 56:8 (MSG) says, "You've kept track of my every toss and turn through the sleepless nights, Each tear entered in your ledger, each ache written in your book."

Secondly, the Bible gives us peace—peace that passes understanding. There were times when I did not know how I functioned as a teacher, came home to take care of my young boys and all the while responding to court and court papers except that peace Jesus gave me peace.

> Peace I leave with you; my peace I give you, I do not give to you as the world gives. Do not let your hearts be troubled and do not be afraid. (John 14:27 NIV)

> The steadfast of mind You will keep in perfect peace, Because he trusts in You. (Isaiah 26:3 NASB)

Thirdly, the Bible helps us grow in our trust in God. I love seeing how God keeps His promises. I love studying how the Old Testament promises are fulfilled in the New Testament. God is still in the business of fulfilling His promises.

Fourth, God's Word convicts us. This may be something we want to avoid! However, sin blocks us from God; we need to daily look at our hearts and let God's word shine upon it to bring to light thoughts, words, or actions that are not pleasing to God. Psalm 119:11(NIV) says, "I have hidden your word in my heart, that I might not sin against you." One time, I was reading through the book of Hosea, which is a very interesting book. Oftentimes, we think some books like Hosea may not be applicable to us. However, as I was reading how Hosea's prostitute wife stepped out on him (to put it nicely), she said, "I will go after my lovers, who give me my food and my water, my wool and my linen, my oil and my drink" (Hosea 2:5 NIV), I thought about how every time I choose something else to fill my life or put my hope in instead of God, I am "stepping out" on Him. I truly am not any better than Hosea's wife! Being someone who had experienced relationship betrayal pain, I thought about how when I chose other things than God, His heart hurts too. Thank You, Jesus, for forgiveness. While convicting, God's Word also extends forgiveness to our wayward hearts. God does not just forgive us, but He wipes our sin from His memory. Psalm 103:12 NIV says, "As far as the east is from the west, so far has he removed our transgressions from us."

Finally, God's Word gives us an eternity perspective. In the end, this earthly life is but a small dot on an infinite line. A pastor did a visual demonstration of this once, and it has remained ingrained in my head. Stringing a line across the sanctuary and he placed a small dot on it, yet even this does not even compare to eternity. The Bible says of God's Word in Isaiah 40:8 (NASB), "The grass withers, the flowers fade, But the word of our God stands forever." Our God promises in Revelation 21:4 (NASB) that one day, "He will wipe away every tear from their eyes; and there will no longer be *any* death; there will no longer be *any* mourning, or crying, or pain; the first things have passed away."

I also encourage you to pay attention to characters you relate with in the Bible. Study their choices and lives. God put all the stories in there for a reason whether as a warning or as an example to follow. I have gained a lot from the reference book *What the Bible*

Is All About: Bible Handbook by Henrietta C. Mears. She gives relevant insight to how the Bible relates to our lives as well as historical perspective.

One story I will share with you of when I have had confirmation of God's Word. We were going to court yet again. I had a decision to make; my children and how they were affected was always foremost in my mind, but I was so weary and questioning myself. There were days I just felt like giving in. Questions flooded my head: What is worth the battle? What things do I let pass? What accusing emails do I respond to? Do I give in? During this time, I was reading through 2 Samuel and came to a rather obscure passage.

> Now after him was Shammah the son of Agee, a Hararite. And the Philistines were gathered into an army where there was a plot of land full of lentils, and the people fled from the Philistines. But he took his stand in the midst of the plot, defended it, and struck the Philistines; and the Lord brought about a great victory. (2 Samuel 23:11–12 NASB)

Shammah was alone in the middle of the field. I felt alone, exposed, out in the open. By this time, my ex-husband had remarried, and it was a two-against-one situation with many mistruths floating around. The lentil crop was like my children I had invested so much time and sacrifice into. So what did Shammah do? He took his stand and stood his ground to protect the field. In a God incident, my counselor later that week, as I was leaving the session, wrote on a scrap of paper, "Stand, wait." I saved that scrap of paper for many years. How did she know? Really she was insightful, but it was God giving me reassurance. Later I found out that the name *Shammah* means "The Lord is there." Shammah was not alone, and neither was I. Dear friend, you are not alone either. You may have days when you feel so alone, but continually remind yourself of Immanuel—"God is with us"—with you. Remind yourself of Jehovah Shammah—"God is there"—going ahead of you into difficult situations.

I believe Bibles are made to be underlined and written in. Write in your Bible; write dates when God speaks His promises to you. Write names next to verses you are praying for yourself and others. I believe a good Bible is one that is marked up and used! I will share one scripture that kept speaking to me for years, which I believe we saw the fulfillment of in the adoption of our daughter. I wrote next to the scripture Psalm 68:5, which says, "God makes a home for the lonely" many times. I wrote "January 2012" next to it as I felt it as a call to my life. Then in November 2014, I wrote, "Help me to remember my call." In August 2015, I marked the verse again. In 2017, our daughter who had moved through four foster homes came to be in her forever home. She was born in 2011, and God was already preparing a home for her.

I will also provide a warning from using God's Word inaccurately as well. In a book on prayer, *Moving Mountains*, author John Elridge speaks to this issue. Sometimes scripture gives us principles, not promises such as much of the Proverbs. When a scripture is a principle, we can lean into it, but we need to understand it is not a binding promise. Quoting from *Moving Mountains*,

> The Scriptures are not a random grab bag of passages we select willy-nilly like a child trick-or-treating; we do need to be careful about that. Simply because God promised David that his heirs would always sit on the throne doesn't mean I can just grab that for my life. The context of a passage will give you clarity on who it is meant for, whether it is a promise or a principle, whether that promise is for every person or for believers or for a moment in history when God was doing something specific with a particular person. (Once again, in our handling of the Word of God, we are growing in maturity.)

> Having offered this word of caution, I do believe the Scriptures are "living and active," that God

can and does apply passages and promises to us
as individuals even though their origins may have
been in different historical moment.

I think I could go on and on about the Bible's importance, but I will stop and let you pick it up. Get to know the God who desires to know you intimately.

Our Minds

For those who are in accord with the flesh set their minds on
the things of the flesh, but those who are in accord with the
Spirit, the things of the Spirit. For the mind set on the flesh
is death, but the mind set on the Spirit is life and peace.
Romans 8:5–7 NASB

We want minds that are life and peace as in the scripture above. Do an analysis of everything that is going into your mind on a daily basis. We may begin our day with prayer and reading God's Word but then encounter the world's thoughts and ways the rest of the day. It is inescapable. Philippians 4 says to dwell on things that are true, honorable, right, pure, lovely, and of good report. It is so important to fill your mind with thoughts of our hope in Jesus.

Choose wisely the music and podcasts you listen to. Choose even more wisely the television shows you may watch. We did not have television channels when my boys were young, so we made selections from the video store (if you are young, you will not remember these stores!) or the library. Because we put thought into it, it was much easier not just to have something on that was not uplifting.

Limit your tech use. Do not look at a bunch of happy families on Facebook. There are many forms of media that I am not familiar with that a new generation has to navigate. Ask yourself the hard questions: Is this type of media bringing me closer to God? Is it making me a more mature Christian or a better parent?

Music is powerful to our thought life as well. That is why lyrics get "stuck" in our heads. If possible, find encouraging worship music to listen to throughout the day. Find that song that speaks to you and play it often. For me for a while, that was "Praise You in the Storm" by Casting Crowns.

I also have a dear friend that made me CDs with songs she thought would lift me up. This was in the simple days of pressing play on the CD player. I miss those days! Speaking of dear friends, pray for friends to walk alongside you in this journey.

Jonathans, Purahs, and Barnabases

Therefore encourage one another and build each
other up, just as in fact you are doing.
1 Thessalonians 5:11 NIV

Here is a little history on Psalm 31 that I have used as guidance in writing this book. The psalm was written by David and according to the Zondervan NIV Study Bible commentary it was, "A prayer for deliverance when confronted by a conspiracy so powerful and open that all David's friends abandoned him. According to Luke 23:46, Jesus on the cross applied Psalm 31:5 to his own circumstances; those who share in his suffering at the hands of anti-Christian forces are encouraged to hear and use this psalm in a new light. No psalm expresses a more sturdy trust in the Lord when powerful human forces threaten."

Here is some of what David shares in Psalms 31.

I'm ridiculed by the neighbors.
My friends are horrified; they cross the street to avoid me.
They want to blot me from memory,
forget me like a corpse in a grave,
discard me like a broken dish in the trash. (MSG)

I am here to tell you that even if divorce was not your choice, there will be friends, Christians even, who begin to avoid you. Divorce strikes a fear in them. Could it be contagious? Were you not a true Christian or godly spouse? Will you try to steal their husband or wife? You will lose relationships for the reason that typically joint relationships—meaning those you shared with your spouse—usually end up choosing a side. I pray for you that you will have friends who stand with you—who support you and speak truth into your lives. Friends who help you not to be bitter but encourage you in God's love. Friends who tell you you can do it and you will get through it. Friends who can give you good counsel.

The church oftentimes does not know what to do with us either. I understand their conundrum, not wanting to condone divorce and yet needing to provide a safe place for healing to occur. It is a difficult line to walk.

Do not feel bad if there are people in your life who you need to limit time with. People who may desire to speak poorly of your ex-spouse in an effort to make you feel better. That is absolutely not what you need. Neither do you need people that condemn you, for not trying hard enough or making mistakes in your marriage. This is also not helpful. We all make mistakes in our marriages; but for some reason, some marriages, even Christian ones, come to an end.

The Bible gives us examples of the kind of friendships we do need, people who walk with us as we follow Jesus. Read of David and Jonathan's friendship in 1 Samuel 18:1–4 and of how Jonathan protected David in 1 Samuel chapters 19 and 20. Some of my Jonathans came in the form of pastors. One who looked out for me when my husband first left and filed for divorce; he took a stand on my and the children's behalf. Another pastor a few years later also took a stand when my ex-husband and his fiancée attempted to come to my home church. They gave me a list of demands, including that I should attend at a different time and I was not allowed to see my sons while they were at church. I went to the pastor, and of course, he rightly said anyone is welcome to church, but he preached a sermon full of conviction on that Sunday.

There is a short passage concerning Gideon in Judges 7. I love Gideon because he was so real. Read about his calling and questioning of God in Judges 6. After God had given Gideon signs and reassurance, it still says in Judges 7:10, "But if you are afraid to go down, go with Purah your servant to the camp." I was fortunate enough to have family (mainly my mom and my sister) close by that went with me to court and to lawyers. They were definitely my "Purahs."

Finally, Barnabas shows up in Acts 4 and is named the "son of encouragement." We all need encouragers in our lives—people who encourage us to grow in God's ways. In Acts 11:22–24 (MSG), it says of Barnabas,

> When the church in Jerusalem got wind of this, they sent Barnabas to Antioch to check on things. As soon as he arrived, he saw that God was behind and in it all. He threw himself in with them, got behind them, urging them to stay with it the rest of their lives. He was a good man that way, enthusiastic and confident in the Holy Spirit's ways. The community grew large and strong in the Master.

When my boys were still young, I met one of my Barnabases, a godly woman a decade younger than me who has walked with me through difficult years as well as joyous moments, always encouraging me in my relationship with Jesus. There was also another friend at church who planned family activities at our church at the time and encouraged me to try new things I would have not done otherwise. A childhood friend has walked life's journey with me since fourth grade, truly a priceless blessing.

I pray that you will have people in your life like this and that one day you will be a Jonathan, a Purah, and a Barnabas to those who God brings in your life. You may not see the light at the end of the tunnel now, but you will get there one day. Jesus is talking to Peter in Luke 22:32 (MSG). First of all, Jesus says He is praying for Peter: "Simon I have prayed for you that you not give in or give out." (What a comfort that Jesus intercedes for us!) Then Jesus says, "When you have come through the time of testing, turn to your companions and give them a fresh start." God will use your circumstances one day to help others.

If you do not feel like you have those kinds of supportive relationships, pray specifically for those kinds of people in your life.

Mostly, always remember that Jesus is the friend who sticks closer than a brother. Even in Jesus's life when he needed his friends, they fell asleep! Who did Jesus turn to? His heavenly Father.

Counselors

Without good direction, people lose their way; the more
wise counsel you follow, the better your chances.
Proverbs 11:14 MSG

Some of your Purahs may come in the form of a counselor. I am a huge proponent of counseling, good counseling anyway. My counselor through the divorce and for many years beyond was a God-send. She provided me with unbiased insight and guided me through years of mediation and court. I am forever grateful. Obviously, the divorce was impactful, but we all have pain from our childhoods and family of origin no matter how well we were raised. This is the opportunity for you to become a healthier person. My counselor moved away eventually. However, after some time and after being remarried, I went back to counseling to work on some more issues I needed to address. I am a healthier person and a stronger Christian because of it. Do not be afraid, embarrassed, or ashamed to get the help you need. I often remember feeling stressed about the time the counseling took or having to get someone to watch the boys, but it is worth the time and effort put in.

This is my detour and side note. That being said, there are as many ungodly counselors as there are good ones. Do not be afraid to shop around for the right fit for you. If something your counselor is saying doesn't sit right or does not jive with biblical wisdom, seek another. I hesitate to even put a section in this book on self-care because I have been to counselors whose only guidance is to do what makes you happy and take care of yourself. I truly believe in stewardship of your body, of your talents. I walk and I eat healthy. I think sugar is a trap that keeps us from being our best. It is so important to move your body in some way and to nourish your brain and creativity. It is important to find activities that relax you. Nevertheless, if your soul is not fed by God, you will find those things empty—simple fixes that do not last. There are also stages in life—times that you will have more time to exercise and times where most of your energy will be devoted to your family. Life is a balancing act, but without Jesus at our center, we will never get that balance right. Put Jesus in the center, and everything else becomes aligned.

God Is Our Provider

The Lord upholds all who fall
And lifts up all who are bowed down
The eyes of all look to you,
And you give them their food at the proper time.
Psalm 145:14–16 NIV

Divorce has a major impact on finances, even if assets are divided equally. For me, I lost health insurance for half of a year and had to humble myself by taking state insurance. We sold our home, and I moved in with my parents for a short time while looking for a home I could afford. I consider myself fortunate that we have saved, made a slight profit on our home, and had a down payment to buy a home. Most likely, you are also in a situation where the economy of your family has changed as well.

I give the story of Hagar as an example of how God provides for us. Hagar's financial situation had definitely changed. She went from living under Abraham's protection and provision to wandering in the desert after Sarah banished her, placing her young son under a bush because she could not watch him die. Grab your Bible and read about how God provided for her and Ishmael in the desert in Genesis 21:8–20. Turn back to Genesis 16 as well and read about how Hagar fled on her own the first time after Sarah had mistreated her. God showed up in the desert this time too. The Bible says, "The angel of the Lord found Hagar near a spring in the desert." The angel of the Lord tells her that the Lord has heard of her misery. Hagar aptly names the well "Beer Lahai Roi," which means "well of the

Living One who sees me." Dear friend, God has found you, hears your prayer, and sees your situation.

God provided a miraculous job for me as I mentioned before. The first time my husband left when Garrett was a toddler, I was at the public library for preschool story time. I still had my teaching contract as I had taken a year-long child-rearing leave. There was a grandma at the library story hour with her grandson who I overheard talking about her daughter needing a job share partner for the same district I worked for. How could this not be God? It was a kindergarten position that I was certified for. Because I was unsure of the direction the marriage was headed, I went back part-time until I became pregnant with Nathan. Nathan was a fall baby, and because I did not desire to start a year with kindergartners and leave the students after two months, I gave up my teaching contract, not knowing what was to be. In spring, when my husband left permanently, the principal hired me back. I call these people like my principal "Cyruses"—people God uses to pave a way for His people. The most miraculous part was, it was a part-time job with health insurance. I was able to continue in this position until Nate was almost four years old. Of course we made financial sacrifices, but it was well worth the time I had with the boys when they were young.

God is watching over you as well. You will have some hard decisions to make. You may have to explain to your children why "wants" have to be prioritized differently. You may have to move. You may have to go back to school or get a new job. None of this will be easy, but as you take each step, God is right there with you.

The Beautiful God Planned Life

And we know that God causes all things to work
together for good to those who love God, to those
who are called according to His purpose.
Romans 8:28 NASB

After my husband left, I painted the word "Hope" on the wall, and I would look at it at night before I went to sleep. This is not just any hope though. If it was hope in my frail humanity, I would be doomed. This is hope in the fact that one day God will set all things right. One day, every knee will bow, and every tongue will confess that Jesus is Lord. This is hope in that God will work all things out for the good of those who love and serve Him. This is the hope that says God is the potter, I am clay, and He is using all things in my life to shape me into a useful vessel for Him.

You may not be able to see His purposes and this is where trusting our Guide comes in. Underline all of Isaiah 55:8–13 (NIV) in your Bible. It begins with, "For my thoughts are not your thoughts, neither are your ways my ways, declares the Lord, so are my ways higher than your ways and my thoughts than your thoughts." It offers promises of when the "rain and snow" come, God has His purpose in it. It will not water the earth without causing something to grow.

While walking in the woods one day, I wondered why trees sometimes have those big knots and yet seem to grow healthy and strong beyond that knot. Upon doing some research, the knots are actually called burls, and they are a reaction to stress. The burl protects the tree like a scar and saves the tree's life. Nevertheless, the burl is prized by woodworkers for its intricate design. We may have burls in our life, but we can continue to thrive, our "burls" used for God's glory and beauty. Ephesians 2:10 (NLT) says, "We are God's masterpiece. He has created us anew in Christ Jesus, so we can do the good things he planned for us long ago."

We may have burls in our life, but we can continue to thrive, our "burls" used for God's glory and beauty.

At the time of my divorce, I could not see the future or what it would hold. I would be a single mom but experience so much joy from raising my boys. I find it a blessing that our relationship was so cemented. Being a single mom for many years has made me so much more independent. I did not know that one day after many years I would be remarried or that my current husband and I would foster and adopt our daughter. Although I would not biologically have more children as I longed for, I would have more children through adoption and the addition of step children.

God is preparing you for the unique purpose He has for your life. Trust his plan. This may be an overused proverb, but nevertheless, it is true. "Trust in the Lord with all your heart, and do not lean on your understanding. In all your ways acknowledge Him and He will make your paths straight" Proverbs 3:5–6 (NASB).

Applications
Chapter 2: Trust Your Guide

1. When is the best time of day for you to meet officially with God? Plan it, have your Bible ready to go in your prayer spot if you are a morning person. Set the coffee to automatically brew in the mornings!

2. What picture brings you reassurance of God's love? For me, it was sitting on Jesus's lap. Even if you are not an artist, sketch a picture below!

3. List all your little and big concerns; remember, nothing is too little for God and nothing is too big. Write them down and turn them over to God. Bookmark this page and every time a worry or concern comes to mind write it down. (If it is your book, earmark pages!)

4. What characters in the Bible speak to you? What is their story? How did they follow God? What mistakes did they make?

5. What are ways you can set your mind "on things above"? What did you need to limit or do away with in your life that keeps you from being your best?

6. Who do you have in your life that is a support? Is there anyone who saps your energy that maybe you need to limit time with?

7. Pray for good counsel. Read the short book of Ruth. Ruth listened to an older, wiser woman and took her counsel.

3

Hidden Traps

Free me from hidden traps
I want to hide in you.
Psalm 31:3–5 MSG

I actually do not want to write this chapter! It takes me back to times that were so difficult, but it is necessary work if we are to be lights and examples to our children. We can use all the correct words, but our children see us as we truly are—beneath those words to our hearts. You cannot hide your true self from them. For that reason, we need to be sure we are being the godly examples they need. During divorce and parenting afterward, you will need to continually check your heart.

Chapter 2 is really all about developing intimacy with God. The definition of an *intimate relationship* from *Merriam-Webster Dictionary* is "marked by a warm friendship developing through long association." The more we are around Jesus, the more we trust Jesus, the more likely we are to be able to accept corrections from Him. When we correct our children, it is because we want the best for them. When Jesus shines light into the corner of our hearts that holds darkness, it is because He wants us to be the best we can be.

> *When Jesus shines light into the corner of our hearts that holds darkness, it is because He wants us to be the best we can be.*

I think of the warning God gives when He gently confronts Cain. Cain's anger is simmering in his heart. God says to him Genesis 4:6–7 (NIV), "Why are you angry? Why is your face downcast? If you do what is right, will you not be accepted? But if you do not do what is right, sin is crouching at your door; it desires to have you, but you must master it." *Moody Bible Commentary* says, "Contrary to what is often thought, Cain is to be regarded as a believer…, and hence one whom the believing reader can relate." It goes to say, "Cain's anger did not immediately vent itself in murder. Instead it moved from the stage of inner enmity to verbal dispute. This is implied by the reference in this verse to Cain 'speaking' with Abel." With Cain as our warning, let's examine the "hidden traps" divorce may bring to the forefront.

Unforgiveness

If I had cherished sin in my heart,
the Lord would not have listened.
Proverbs 66:18 NASB

The first hidden trap is unforgiveness. You may have been truly wronged and feel like you deserve the righteous anger box in your soul, but eventually, it will destroy your own soul. Bitterness is just plain ugly. Proverbs 27:19 (MSG) says, "Just as water mirrors your face so your face mirrors your heart." This does not mean it is an easy journey. This does not mean we should deny our emotions. It does mean we need to work toward being in a place where we realize we are sinners in need of God's grace as much as any other human on this earth. We need to open the box and deal with its contents. I looked up every verse in the Bible on forgiveness and wrote it in my journal. However, forgiving was not a one-time event. You will still, for the sake of your children, need to deal with an ex-spouse. I pray it will be an easy road for you, but often it is not. I had to make forgiveness a daily effort.

The Bible, as always, does not leave us without examples of forgiveness with the ultimate example being that of Christ on the cross.

"But Jesus was saying, 'Father forgive them; for they do not know what they are doing'" (Luke 23:34 NASB). Jesus was practicing what He taught. And why was Jesus able to do this? It tells us in 1 Peter it was because He trusted and entrusted Himself to God. The entirety of the verses say,

> For you have been called for this purpose, because Christ also suffered for you, leaving you an example, so that you would follow in His steps, He who committed no sin, nor any deceit found in His mouth; and while being abusively insulted, He did not insult in return; while suffering, He did not threaten, but kept entrusting Himself to Him who judges righteously. (1 Peter 2:21–23 NASB)

This is why chapter 2 is so important, trusting God will lead to forgiving others. I like the words "kept entrusting." We need to follow Jesus's example and keep entrusting our lives to the One who loves us so much He gave His own Son's life. There was one time I remember my ex-husband saying to me, "I know people in high places." I remember replying but "I know the person in the highest place." That is where my trust is.

Whitewashed Walls

> Therefore everyone who hears these words
> of mine and puts them into practice is like
> a wise man who built his house on the rock.
> The rain came down, the streams rose, and the
> winds blew and beat against that house; yet it
> did not fall, because it had its foundation on
> the rock. But everyone who hears these words
> of mine and does not put them into practice
> is like a foolish man who built his house
> on sand. The rain came down, the streams

> rose, and the winds blew and beat against
> that house, and it fell with a great crash.
> Matthew 7:24–27 NIV

As much as unforgiveness is detrimental to our own health, something I title "pseudo-forgiveness" is just as destructive. What I mean by this is pretending to forgive when we really have not. Christians are especially in danger of this because we think it is what we "should do" or feel and possibly because we desire to look good to other Christians around us.

The book of Ezekiel is a book of warning of falsehood of which I think we can take heed. Chapter 13 verse 5 (NIV) warns the prophets, "You have not gone up to the breaches in the wall to repair it." Rather, the prophets had whitewashed the wall. The definition of whitewash is to gloss over or cover up. Part of verse 10 reads,

> Peace, when there is no peace, and because, when a flimsy wall is built, they cover it with whitewash, therefore tell those who cover it with whitewash that it is going to fall. Rain will come in torrents, and I will send hailstones hurtling down, and violet winds will burst forth. When the wall collapses, will not people ask you, "Where is the whitewash you covered it with?"

Scary! God wants to be honest with our feelings. If it is hard, pour your heart out to Him.

Consider the story of Joseph. This story is often glossed over, seemingly that Joseph had no emotion and just forgave. Look again at the details of this story in Genesis. Begin reading in Genesis 37 of how Joseph's own brothers sold him, rejected him. Joseph was not innocent exactly, as none of us are. He was rather an arrogant young man, but God used all things in his life to shape him into an example for us. Read chapters 40 and 41. Joseph did not become bitter, but I am sure he dealt with the emotion of being rejected by his family and coming to a place where he could see God's hand with him. We know his steward acknowledges Joseph's God when addressing the brothers, and we can deem Joseph lived out his faith.

As the text continues through chapter 45, we do not know exactly what Joseph was thinking, but it does tell us that he wept three times. First in chapter 42:24 (NIV), "He turned away from them and began to weep," and again in chapter 43:30, "Deeply moved at the sight of his brother, Joseph hurried out and looked for a place to weep." Finally, he weeps again in chapter 45 when he reveals himself to his brothers. Joseph is an example for us. He did not hide or deny his emotion, at least not in front of God. We need to do this as well, definitely before God and possibly with a counselor or someone that will encourage us to process our pain and use our circumstances to grow.

The second example of forgiveness we need to take from Joseph is he did not jump back into a relationship with his brothers. He exercised caution; he was gentle as a dove and wise as a serpent. Obviously, we should not put people to tests as Joseph did, but we need to be thoughtful and wise. The *Moody Bible Commentary* says, "Although it might seem as if Joseph toyed with his brothers, in reality he was testing them. These interactions were designed to evaluate their consciences, their character, and their compassion, all traits sorely lacking when they sold him into slavery." We can forgive and still be wise and discerning. A relationship with our ex-spouse is going to look very different than functioning as a married couple. We are going to have different boundaries to navigate.

There is one verse that I would repeat to myself when my ex-husband came to pick up the children. He often made it clear that he was leaving me, not the children. I would repeat in my head what Joseph said to his brothers Genesis 50:19 (NASB): "Don't be afraid. Am I in the place of God? You intended to harm me, but God intended it for good to accomplish what is now being done, the saving of many lives."

There are whole books written on the topic of forgiveness with much more detail than I cover here. Visit my website for a list of printable forgiveness scriptures and see recommendations at the end of the book for further reading. I will end with this section with an excerpt from the book *Boundaries* by Dr. Henry Cloud:

> Nothing clarifies boundaries more than forgiveness. To forgive someone means to let him off the hook, or to cancel a debt he owes you. When you refuse to forgive someone, you still want something from that person, and even if it is revenge that you want, it *keeps you tied to him forever.*

Anger and Revenge

> Do not take revenge, my dear friends, but leave
> room for God's wrath, for it is written, 'It is
> mine to avenge; I will repay,' says the Lord.
> Romans 12:19 NIV

Anger is a natural human emotion. Jesus is with you in your anger. I am going to quote from a book I highly recommend, *Gentle and Lowly, The Heart of Christ for Sinners and Sufferers.* Author Dane Ortlund says this way more beautifully and eloquently than I ever could.

> Are you angry today? Let us not be too quick to assume our anger is sinful. After all, the Bible positively orders us to be angry when occasion calls for it (Ps. 4:4, Eph. 4:26). Perhaps you have reason to be angry. Perhaps you have been sinned against, and the only appropriate response is anger. Be comforted by this: *Jesus is angry alongside you.* He joins you in your anger. Indeed, he is angrier than you could ever be about the wrong done to you. Your just anger is a shadow of his. And his anger, unlike yours, has zero taint of sin in it. As you consider those who have wronged you, let Jesus be angry on your behalf. His anger

can be trusted. For it an anger that springs from his compassion for you. The indignation he felt when he came upon the mistreatment of others in the Gospels is the same indignation he feels now in heaven upon mistreatment of you.

In that knowledge, release your debtor and breathe again. Let Christ's heart for you not only wash you in his compassion but also assure you of his solidarity in rage against all that distresses you, most centrally death and hell.

Let us also look at the wise example of Abigail who kept David from seeking his own revenge. Read the entirety of 1 Samuel 25 and meet me back here for a discussion!

We find intelligent, beautiful Abigail married to a harsh, foolish man Nabal. When Nabal insults David, David is going to take revenge. David's anger is controlling him. He definitely was not taking the time to consult God. Thank goodness for the calm, collected Abigail. She reminds David of the Lord's work in his life and the plans God has for David's future. David listens to her and says in verse 33, "May you be blessed for your good judgment and for keeping me from bloodshed this day and from avenging myself with my own hands." Let us live out the Proverb 12:15 (NIV) as David did, "The way of fools seems right to them, but the wise listen to advice."

David gets credit for listening to Abigail, but let us also look at Abigail's life. Although Abigail was married to a man the Message version calls brutish, mean, and impossible, she exercised good judgment and wisdom. How did she live with such a husband and not let it change her character? Abigail had a choice and so do we. While Nabal had no concern for his herdsman and family under his care, Abigail fought to save those under her care. She was focused on what really mattered. We can focus on what really matters as well—our children. Abigail also had faith in God, fear of God, and believed in God as witnessed in the speech she made to David. The speech is one of the longest recorded by a woman and also noted as one the wisest speeches made in scripture. Abigail acknowledges how God has been with David and predicts how God will continue to be with David. She references that David fights the Lord's battles. Similarly, we need to choose our battles carefully and wisely. David blesses Abigail's "discernment." With those examples, let us move to the power of words. We may not be fighting battles like David, but our words can be used to exact revenge as well.

Power of Spoken Words

> With the tongue we praise our Lord and
> Father, and with it we curse men, who have
> been made in God's likeness. Out of the same
> mouth come praise and cursing. My brothers,
> this should not be. Can both fresh water
> and salt water flow from the same spring?
> James 3:9–11 NIV

We need to be careful with our words. I recall a time when the toilet was clogged, and I was trying to get the boys to bed at a decent time while just wanting just to crawl into bed myself, and Nate in pure innocence as a boy of three years old said, "I know Daddy could fix it." I wanted to scream, "But your dad is not here! He left us." I thank God that he put a muzzle over my mouth. Number one, every three-year-old boy should think of his dad as a hero. It puzzled me because Nate never knew what it was like to have parents who lived together, and yet somehow, he felt like that was what a dad should do. What good would there have been for Nate if I said anything negative? Would it have changed the circumstance or brought anything good for him or me to the situation? I promise there will be many times that you will need to hold your tongue; many times you will have to weigh if the words you want to say will bring life or death.

Although I do not recall where I read this, I am grateful I learned the principle early on. When you speak of the person who biologically brought your child into the world with you in a negative light, your child who feels a like part of them, feels that criticism in their soul as well. This absolutely does not mean you should lie or hide the truth, but in almost all cases, there are positive attributes your child has that they received from that ex-spouse. Things I would say to my boys would be "you have math minds just like your dad." I have a horrible sense of direction. Both boys get an excellent sense of direction from their dad. They have kept me many times from being completely lost!

You married your ex-spouse for a reason. At some point, you saw good in them, and hopefully, you can recall some of those traits and share them with your child. This is not everyone's circumstance, but I am grateful that I can honestly tell the boys, "I would be married to your dad all over again just to have you." The marriage ended, but there were good times and we were friends at one time. I can tell them the good experiences that I did share with their dad.

Please understand I am not recommending living in a fairy land of make-believe. Truth reigns, but we need to be discerning about our child's age and maturity level and readiness to hear the truth. Your child will experience their own journey to healing and they may need to know some difficult facts along the way. Your job is to walk beside them and gently give them the information they need at the right time. Ask God for wisdom each step of the way.

When you do need to vent about an ex-spouse, go to God, go to a counselor, go to an Abigail-like friend, but do not be tempted to engage in these conversations with your children.

Older Brother Syndrome

His father said to him, "Look, dear
son, you have always stayed by me,
and everything I have is yours."
Luke 15:31 NLT

When I study the story of the prodigal son, I always feel some sympathy for the older brother. Here he was working away for his father, doing the right thing day in and day out. At least, from outward appearances, he was. The condition of his heart was a different story. When he saw how his father treated his brother when he returned after squandering his money, he was angry. I honestly think, in my humanness, I would be angry too! Oh no, here is the anger word again! So also is the warning.

Therefore, I do have to explore the topic, how would I feel if my son's dad returned to God? Even more so, how would I feel if a step parent who has continually overstepped boundaries, comes to know God? And ugh, am I praying for them?

Let us once again turn to God's Word. Matthew 5 contains the well-known verse about loving your enemies.

> You have heard that it was said, "You shall love your neighbor and hate your enemy." But I say to you, love your enemies and pray for those who persecute you, so that you may prove yourselves to be sons of your Father who is in heaven; for He causes His sun to rise on *the* evil and *the* good, and sends rain on *the* righteous and *the* unrighteous. For if you love those who love you, what reward do you have? Even the tax collectors, do they not do the same? (Matthew 5:43–46 NIV)

Sometimes, God asks us to do very difficult things, but not on our own strength, only through his strength. I came to a point where I had to ask myself, "What would be best for my sons?" Do I want them to have the reassurance that one day their dad will be with them in heaven? "Sigh," I do.

Even more importantly, what does God desire? The Matthew excerpt above ends with "Be perfect, therefore, as your heavenly Father is perfect." My will should be aligned with His will. His Word tells us what His will is. The Old Testament verse from Ezekiel 33:11 (NASB) says, "I take no pleasure in the death of the wicked, but rather that they turn from their ways and live." The New Testament says in 2 Peter 3:9 (NIV), "The Lord is not slow in keeping his promise, as some understand slowness. Instead He is patient with you, not wanting anyone to perish, but everyone to come to repentance."

There is another biblical account I like to refer to that reminds us to keep our focus on Jesus. It is in the last chapter of the book of John, Jesus has returned and appeared to his disciples for the third time after the resurrection. Although you may want to read the whole chapter of John 21 for greater context, the conversation between Jesus and Peter begins in verse 15. I draw two truths from this story. The first is to stay focused on our mission. Jesus is asking Peter if he loves him; and Peter, of course, responds, "Yes, Lord, you know I love you." Jesus asks Peter for a total of three times with Peter responding in the positive. Jesus replies three times with "Feed my lambs," "Shepherd my sheep," and "Feed my sheep." Those we have in our care, our lambs, are our children, first and foremost. That is our focus, their best interest is what we work for. The story continues revealing the second truth. Peter, who is a little frustrated after the third time Jesus questions him and probably not quite comprehending what Jesus is telling him loses his focus.

Those we have in our care, our lambs, are our children, first and foremost. That is our focus, their best interest is what we work for.

"Turning his head," Peter takes his eyes off of Jesus physically and emotionally and asks—what Jesus has in store for John. Jesus basically says, "What's that to you? You—follow me." Therein lies the second truth and brings us back to the guide metaphor. Follow Jesus, keep your eyes on him, and focus on the mission he has specifically for you.

Dear friend, I am almost eighteen years out from my divorce, so as I write this, it may seem I have oversimplified this. If you are in the thick of things, it may not seem possible to pray for an ex-spouse. In all honesty, there are days I still battle this. As you study God's Word and abide in Him, He will give you the right verses to pray. Max Lucado writes in his book *Anxious for Nothing* that your job is not to bear fruit. Your job is to cling to Jesus. Hold on to Him and fruit will grow. It is not a one-day fix—it is a constant taking up of our cross and following Jesus.

Lawyers and Courts

For their Defender is strong, he will
take up their case against you.
Proverbs 23:11 NIV

You may wonder why I put this topic under hidden traps. I pray you have a Christian lawyer who works in the best interest for you and mostly for your children. This was not necessarily the case for me. I felt caught in a trap with lawyers on both sides whose focus seemed to be to have drama with each other. At one point, I had to let my lawyer go and find someone who I felt was more rational and exercised better judgment. By this time, my boys were older, and I wish it was something I had done sooner.

I cringe when I think of the money spent over the years on lawyers, I wonder how I was even able to pay. God, somehow, in His providence, made sure I always had enough. The whole system is set up to protect children, but it is also a very flawed system. As I mentioned, we were in court so much that the court eventually assigned us a mediator. This was definitely something positive that came out of an imperfect system.

The experience of being in the courtroom where you feel like you have no power over the fate of your children is overwhelming. The judge is arbitrarily making a decision that affects you and your children with very limited knowledge. This gave me great anxiety, and I found comfort in the verses that gave me a visual picture of how God was with me and went with me. When I taught reading to kindergarteners, one of the skills I taught students was mental imagery. When I read a text without pictures, they created the picture in their head. Using mental imagery while reading can improve comprehension. While reading God's Word, it is helpful to visualize the ways in which He promises to protect us and go with us. It can help us comprehend how much God loves us.

You hem me in behind and before; you have laid
your hand upon me. (Psalm 139:5 NIV)

Many are the woes of the wicked, but the Lord's unfailing love surrounds the man who trusts in him. (Psalm 32:10 NIV)

The angel of the Lord encamps around those who fear him, and he delivers them. (Psalm 34:7 NIV)

When you pass through the waters, I will be with you; And through the rivers, they will not over-flow you. When you walk through the fire, you will not be scorched, Nor will the flame burn you. For I am The Lord your God, The Holy One of Israel, your Savior. (Isaiah 55:2–3 NASB)

But you will not leave in haste or go in flight; for the Lord will go before you, the God of Israel will be your rear guard. (Isaiah 52:12 NIV)

I have put my words in your mouth and covered you with the shadow of my hand—I who set the heavens in place, who laid the foundations of the earth, and who say to Zion, "You are my people." (Isaiah 58:16 NASB)

Even if you physically have to go to court alone, have a picture in your head of how Jesus is going before you and surrounding you with his love and strength.

Finally, the court system does not bring out the best in people. When one side is trying to make the other side look bad or at least make themselves look better, they resort to all sorts of tactics. You may have to defend yourself at times, but resist the urge to strike back with anything but truth. The Message version of Matthew 10:16 says, "Be as cunning as a snake, inoffensive as a dove." There were times to respond and times to let things go. Psalm 41:10 in the KJV says, "But thou, O Lord, be merciful unto me, and raise me up, that I may requite them." *Requite* can mean to give something back or something in return. The NIV text note says to "call them to account." There are battles to be fought, battles to let go of. There are times to stand your ground and times to let things go.

There were oftentimes I had to let go of my reputation and leave it in God's hands. Look at 1 Peter 2:23 (MSG) again, always using Jesus as our example, "They called him every name in the book and he said nothing back. He suffered in silence, content to let God set things right." Hopefully, for most families, much is settled in the initial court process. For me, it lasted for years with the only goal I often had was to come out with my integrity intact, to be the example God called me to be for my sons.

> Guard my soul and save me;
> Do not let me be ashamed, for I take refuge in You.
> Let integrity and uprightness protect me,
> For I wait for You.
> Psalm 25:20–21 NASB

Comments That Cut

> Careless words stab like a knife,
> But wise words bring healing.
> Proverbs 12:18 NCV

Life has many awkward situations where we struggle on what is appropriate to say to people who are in the midst of difficult circumstances. I cannot count the times I have wondered why I made an ill-suited comment to a friend or acquaintance about a certain circumstance. That is why I can extend grace to others who in an effort to encourage me sometimes said some rather hurtful things to me concerning my divorce. They were well intentioned, but sometimes the comments sting. Do not let these comments spiral you downward.

One of the first comments I heard was from a woman at church who blatantly said I could never get married again or I would be committing adultery. I was thirty-two at the time, and although not considering remarriage anytime soon, I know I longed for marriage and more children. I am not going to debate the scriptural context she used here. I was actually able to consider the source and turn it over to the One who is my source.

This next comment came from my dear mom who I love and admire and who has walked with me through trials all these years. She just happened to use the word "broken family" to describe us. Because we have a good relationship, I was eventually able to tell her how that made me feel. Living under the canopy of the word "broken" is not a good word picture! Even intact families have brokenness. This is God's promise for all of us. Consider the words of Jesus as He was talking to His disciples before He went back to heaven. The Message version of John 14:25–27 says, "The Friend, the Holy Spirit whom the Father will send at my request, will make everything plain to you. He will remind you of all the things I have told you. I'm leaving you well and whole. That's my parting gift to you." God leaves us "whole" and "well," not broken. Interestingly enough to me, when one's spouse passes away, we do not call the family a "broken family." You may have a different composition, but you are still a family. In the next section of the book, I will discuss concrete ways of rebuilding your family.

"The Friend, the Holy Spirit whom the Father will send at my request, will make everything plain to you. He will remind you of all the things I have told you. I'm leaving you well and whole. That's my parting gift to you."

The following comment was made to me on more than one occasion. I would run into another mom at a store, and they would comment on how nice it must be to shop without my children or how nice it must be to get a break from my children. I never really wanted a "break" from my children. When they left on their dad's time, I would feel a deep ache in my heart that did not leave until they were home. When they were gone, I had little knowledge of what they were doing or who they were with. I understand the busyness of motherhood or fatherhood and breaks are good when we need them; I just had a different perspective on "breaks."

Following that comment, there was a comment of how when I had my "break." I must have had time to take a bath or do something nice for myself. In reality, I had the job of two parents. All the chores that used to be divided fell solely on me. Due to my teaching career, much of my "break" time was spent lesson planning. I had to wash, cook, grocery shop, clean the house in addition to doing the bills, mowing the lawn, fixing, and maintaining the house. All of which, at times, overwhelmed me.

This following comment I actually agree with, but it was what people did not see behind the scenes. "It's good their dad is still in their lives." It is good, and I would not have it any other way. However, transitions were horrible for my children. They had to adjust to two different homes, rules, and styles of parenting. I seem to get all the anger, emotion, and sadness the boys had; and I had to deal with it on my own. I will say it again: This is why it is so important for us to be dealing with our own emotions—so that we can be there when our children need us to be strong for them.

This leads to the comment that my children are fine because they did well in public and school settings. However, when I was home with my three-year-old on days off, and he would mention his dad every five minutes, I saw the insecurity he had of going back and forth between two parents. When my oldest would wonder at night if when he woke up I would still be there, my heart ached for him. When one of my sons was a little older and had an unexplained period of anger, I actually think he was grieving the divorce.

Another comment I received was that in the long run, it was probably better for the children rather than living in a home with conflict. There is an excellent book written by Elizabeth Maquardt titled *Between Two Worlds: The Inner Lives of Children of Divorce*. The author is from a divorced home herself and went on to research and interview over 1,500 young adults. She reports her findings in this book. Marquardt found that only in the case of high-conflict divorces where there is "physical abuse or serious and frequent quarreling" do children fare better after the divorce. However, two-thirds of marriages that end in divorce are considered low-conflict and children fared worse after the divorce. This is not to discourage, but we are empowered when we acknowledge truth.

Then there was "You look great," usually followed by "Are you dating?" I was overall doing fine, but sometimes I was so lonely, it hurt. I missed the emotional support even more than the physical support. I wanted to discuss the cute, wonderful things my kids were doing and the difficulties they had with someone who loved them as much as I did. I wanted someone to help me make decisions about finances or where to go on vacation. To address the dating part, I was so busy, so apprehensive about bringing anyone in my boys' lives, not to mention that I worked in a predominantly female work profession, that dating was very much on the back burner.

Finally…the clincher. "Men—at least you don't have to deal with one." What? I wanted to be married. I wanted to deal with "one." I accepted my husband's quirks and your spouse obviously accepts yours or he would still not be with you. My husband chose to leave me in spite of the fact, though far from perfect, I worked hard to be a good wife.

Between Two Worlds aptly has a section titled "Divorce Happy Talk as Denial." Elizabeth Marquardt's focus is on the children, but I do believe it applies to adults as well, at least to the adults who truly accept the impact divorce has on their children. Quoting from this section of the book,

> Divorce happy talk is our culture's attempt to reconcile two competing desires: the desire to accept widespread divorce and the desire to raise happy, healthy children. These two desires are in direct conflict. To date, the culture's main way of confronting this conflict has been denial in the form of happy talk.

We need to be honest on how divorce affects us and our children. Truth sets us free. When the wind and waves come in the form of comments from people who may not truly understand your circumstances, keep your eyes on Jesus who does understand. Take His hand. He will hold you above the waves. He will shelter you from the wind.

Relationship Rescue…*Not!*

> Keep vigilant watch over your heart;
> that's where life starts.
> Don't talk out of both sides of your mouth;
> avoid careless banter, white lies, and gossip.
> Keep your eyes straight ahead;
> ignore all sideshow distractions.
> Watch your step,
> and the road will stretch out smooth before you.
> Look neither right nor left;
> leave evil in the dust.
> Proverbs 4:23–27 MSG

Jumping into another relationship or remarriage too soon can have disastrous results. Second and third marriages statistically end in divorce more frequently than first marriages. God may have remarriage down the road for you, but please, please exercise caution for your own heart and for the sake of your children. Take the time to do the hard work of knowing if you meet someone or if you do not meet someone, you are confident of who you are in Christ.

I was a single parent for nine years before marrying my husband. There were oftentimes I asked God why I had not met anyone yet, especially as I was nearing forty and knew biologically I would not have more children. However, those years with my boys were irreplaceable. I am glad I did not have the distractions around me and was able to focus on their needs. At the same time, I looked around at remarriage happening for others and felt tinges of jealousy and discontent. In the end, God knew the right timing. I needed to trust Him.

That said, I feel I do need to mention, I have also learned from experience. My husband was not far out of his divorce before we remarried. Looking back, we agree, waiting would have been beneficial for all involved. Although God put us together, we kept running into each other in many different places! Hindsight tells us we could have slowed down, and there may have been less issues that were confronted shortly after marriage.

Marriage is hard work. Blending families is even harder work. If you think someone is going to replace your ex-spouse in your children's life, I am very sorry to tell you, they will not. As much as my husband is a mentor for my children, he is not their father and never will be. He loves them both, and they have a good relationship, but he is not their father. I think of him as their "Paul." Paul was a skilled tentmaker by trade. My husband, Ryan, is multitalented and has been able to teach my sons many new skills. He was a runner in high school and able to come alongside my cross-country running son. Ryan is a hunter and fisherman and taught and passed those skills onto Nate. Ryan and Nate are "buddies" who learned together to kayak fish. They are now planning to learn fly fishing together.

Those are all wonderful gifts from God. However, there will always be some bittersweetness of not sharing your child in the same way as a married couple would. That is why we so need Jesus who loves our children more than we ever could and has their best interest at heart. (I do realize there are cases where fathers or mothers are out of the picture, and the stepparent may be the one who truly fulfills that role. Just think; Joseph was actually Jesus's stepfather.)

My husband actually gave me a blender when he proposed to me. It was cute and symbolic, but Ron Deal, author of *The Smart Stepfamily*, warns that bringing two families together is more like cooking in a crockpot than a blender. Considering this, I use the word *blended* with caution. Back to a child's perspective, Marquardt writes…

> But while the term blended family may name the
> experience or hopes of the adults, when it is used
> to describe children's lives it is just another form
> of happy talk. Our experience was anything but
> blended.

However blended our parents might have felt or hoped to become in their new marriages, as children we always had two families, quite often with members who did not even know each other. After a divorce and remarriage our reality was *divided* not blended.

If this seems harsh, please realize my only goal is to spare you and your children from further heartache. If you do meet that person who seems to fit with you and your children, get godly counsel and do not rush in. "The wise are cautious and avoid danger; fools plunge ahead with reckless confidence" (Proverbs 14:16 NLT).

Missing the Blessings

Then their eyes were opened
and they recognized Him.
Luke 24:31 NASB

There will be blessings along this road to healing you are walking, but it is so easy to miss them when we are in crisis or survival mode. I encourage you to keep a gratitude journal. Although my ex-husband was not there to share my son's first word, guess what he did say his first word! And went on to be very verbal. There are so many signs of God's goodness around us.

There is a story recorded in the gospel of Luke chapter 24 titled the Road to Emmaus. Two disciples were talking about what had occurred concerning Jesus's death, and Jesus himself came up and walked along with them. Only they did not recognize Him! They convey to Jesus all that has happened concerning his death, and Jesus points them to the scripture and explains all the prophecies concerning Himself. They press Jesus to stay and eat with them. It isn't until He blesses and breaks the bread that their eyes are opened, and they recognize Him.

There are many blessings I have recorded over the years, but I recently reread this one in my journal. I started a yearly tradition of biking a certain bike trail, just the boys and I, while on vacation in

Door County with extended family. The past year was a particularly difficult one. Their dad had gone back to court for more custody. Before the bike ride, I fleetingly asked God to provide a deer along the trail. The boys loved wildlife. Biking along, we happened to see a turkey, which was cool for the boys. I sometimes have a continuing conversation with God in my head, so I was like "Wow, thank You, God, You answered, not with a deer, but a turkey." Not long after seeing the turkey, a deer was alongside the path. So in my conversation with God, I was like, "You have given me double blessings." Now if we had not seen any wildlife, it is not like I would have lost my faith! However, I do think when we are open, God is especially tender with us. He was this day. We have now yearly biked the same trail for more than fifteen years, and I think of this every time we are on the trail. And I think of what a double blessing my two sons are. The name of my second son is Nathan, and his name means "gift of God." If you recall, my ex-husband had initially left after Garrett was born, and if we had not reconciled for a period, there would be no Nathan. They are my double blessing. To this day, the boys are still okay doing family time biking with us, and that is a blessing as well!

Live your life with your eyes wide open. Jesus is walking right next to you; don't miss Him and don't miss His hand in even the smallest blessing. This leads us to the second section of this book, one of our greatest blessings, our children.

Applications
Chapter 3: Hidden Traps

1. What are you "hiding" from God? Confess it so that nothing stands between you and God.

    "If I had cherished sin in my heart, the Lord would not have listened" (Psalm 66:18 NIV).

2. What hidden traps did you relate the most to?

3. Where are you in the process of forgiveness? Be honest with God because He already knows; pour out your heart to Him.

4. Are you able to trust and keep entrusting your life to God?

5. Are you able to think of some positive traits your ex had that you can share with your child/children?

6. What kind of "Abigail" wisdom do you need today?

7. Are you able to pray for your ex? If nothing else, pray for your child to have a connection that is positive with your ex if that is possible in your situation. I know it is not healthy in every situation. Then I would pray for Jesus to fill the gaps left in your child's life.

8. What word pictures from scripture speak the most to you? Draw your word picture here.

Don't miss the daily blessings! List your blessings here and start a thankfulness journal.

YOUR CHILD'S STORY

Open your mouth for the
people who cannot speak
For the rights of all the unfortunate.
Open your mouth, judge righteously,
And defend the rights of the poor and needy.
Proverbs 31:8–9 NASB

This section is where my heart is stirred. Who are truly the victims of divorce? It is the children who have had no say in what happens to them, what homes they live in, or how they travel back and forth. It is the children who have to navigate two homes, two sets of rules and expectations. This chapter should have been the first one. However, if you, as a parent, are not first grounded in Jesus as your foundation, you are not going to be able to give your child the support they need. We, as parents, need to be able to listen to our children's stories.

Back to the book *Between Two Worlds*, I think every divorced parent should read it. It was not an easy read for me, but I desired to understand how my children would grow up feeling. Here are two quotes from the book that bring us into our child's realities.

Aiming for a "good divorce" might help adults
feel better about their decision to divorce, or

about the divorce that has been thrust upon them, but the stories of children of divorce show that it is wrong and misleading to describe our experience as "good."

I want to shake loose those glaringly wrong assumptions: That divorce doesn't matter if parents get along. That divorce doesn't matter if the kids don't look like damaged goods. That divorce doesn't matter as long as parents keep loving their children. I believe that all adults—whatever their own history—should be able to tolerate hearing the children's point of view.

I think we should do more than tolerate hearing their view. We should offer compassion and understanding as well. I encourage you to actually buy a copy of the book *Between Two Worlds*. You may want to refer back to it as your child grows. You may want to share portions with your child to open up conversations about how they may feel. It may be helpful for them to know others have felt this way.

This is not to discourage you! Where is our hope? Our hope is in Jesus who defies statistics, who uses all things in our life for good—my favorite verse is Romans 8:28. However, if we gloss over the issues, we cannot address them. So hold these two things in balance, divorce brings certain realities, *and* God is bigger than all our realities.

So hold these two things in balance, divorce brings certain realities, and God is bigger than all our realities.

I wrote this in one of my journals: "My all-time favorite verse that I found shortly after I was divorced follows. I grieved at the sadness, the confusion, and even the anger my three-year-old felt. I grieved that my six-month-old would never know what an intact family felt like. God comforted me with this verse as I put my children's names in it and prayed it almost daily for a while. I still return to it as my younger son grows and cycles through the grieving process he may have not understood as an infant."

> Bestow on Garrett and Nate a crown of beauty
> instead of ashes
> The oil of gladness instead of mourning
> A garment of praise instead of despair
> Garrett and Nate will be called oaks of
> righteousness
> A planting of the Lord
> For the display of His splendor
> From Isaiah 61:3–4 (NIV)

My Son's Stories

> Each heart knows its own bitterness,
> And no one else can share its joy.
> Proverbs 14:10 NIV

I am proud to introduce you to my sons and thank them for letting me share a tender part of their lives. I want to start by saying from the outside no one would know that they have internal struggles regarding the divorce, but they do. They have grown into well-adjusted young men. I honestly give all the glory to God and claim a scripture I started praying for them when they were very young. "All your sons will be taught by the Lord; And the well being of your sons will be great" (Isaiah 54:13 NASB).

They both were model students who did well socially and academically. They did what they were supposed to, got good grades, were respectful to adults, began jobs at sixteen and have worked hard since. Each excelled in a sport in high school. Our mediator used to say they are "all-American kids."

Garrett from a young age was very intellectual and bright. He kept me on my toes, and we both say if I had not been strict with him, he would be a different child! But he did well with structure and boundaries. Academics came easy for him, and he was placed in enrichment in his early years. Garrett discovered a love of running and went on to high school to be a state-level track and cross-country runner. In college now, he is majoring in materials and science engineering.

Garrett called me his second year of college and expressed that although he knew he had everything materially growing up and even knew his dad and I loved him, something was missing. The divorce and living in two worlds had left scars on his soul. He felt like this should not bother him, and he should just get on with life and be grateful for what he had. From his discouraged state, he was brave enough to seek out the help of a counselor. Seeking help is a sign of inner strength, not weakness. It was not a long and drawn-out process, but counseling helped him process through some emotions that were real. As he moves through life, gets married, and has children, I am sure he will have more to process. As much as I wish I could rescue my sons from emotional pain, my prayer, above and beyond, is that they themselves deal with it to bring true healing in the depth of their souls. My prayer is that they use it to grow and touch others' lives.

Nate also did well in school and was constantly praised for his character from elementary to high school. He was and is a leader who treats everyone fairly. He went on to become a star football player, playing varsity as a sophomore—first team all-conference in our town his senior year. Nate is a hard worker and completed an apprenticeship with a concrete company during high school. Nate loves the outdoors, hunting, and fishing. Nate is getting a degree in arboriculture/urban forestry.

My heart broke for Nate because in those formative years of attachment when he should have had a mom and a dad, he could never have them both at the same time. Going back and forth as an infant and toddler left unseen scars on his heart. There was no way for him to express with words at that time how he felt. I watched him go through mourning and the grieving process in his later elementary years. However, he used his pain to become a strong leader for others, to stand up for his beliefs in action and in word when necessary. I have the utmost respect for him as a Christian. He is not perfect and has his struggles as we all do. His senior year of high school, he also sought out a counselor to process his pain from childhood that was starting to seep into his adult life.

All of us have internal struggles whether we came from a divorced home or not, but when we gloss over (remember white-washed walls) and ignore what divorce does to children so we can feel better as adults, we are missing the mark. We are devaluing their pain and stunting their emotional growth.

What Your Children Need to Know about Divorce

The Sovereign Lord has given me
a well-instructed tongue,
to know the word that sustains the weary.
He wakens me morning by morning,
wakens my ear to listen like
one being instructed.
Isaiah 50:4 NIV

We need to have compassion and understanding for our children as they grow up in these two worlds. Here is how author Marquardt describes it: "In other words, after the divorce the task that once belonged to the parents—to make sense of their two differ-ent worlds-becomes the child's. The grown-ups can no longer man-age the challenge, so the child is asked to try."

So poignant, what we as adults could not fix, we now have the expectation for our children to manage. Before we go on, there are few understandings your child needs to have as we help them navi-gate their new world.

First of all, they need to know the divorce was not their fault. It was an adult decision that definitely had and continues to have implications for their life, but there was nothing they could do or not do to; it was not their responsibility to fix a marriage between two adults.

Secondly, they need to know you will help them manage the changes. Children often now have two places to live. As much as you can, put yourself in your child's shoes. Personally, as an introvert who likes consistency, I cannot imagine carting my "stuff" back and forth. I cannot imagine sleeping in two different beds. I cannot imagine changing my mindset to accommodate each household's standards every few days. Calendars can help children know ahead of time where they are going and relieve some anxiety. Having a peaceful, consistent household so your child knows what to expect when they come home can also go a long way to ease anxiety.

Thirdly, when children are in two homes, carrying their "stuff" back and forth is a burden. This was a huge conflict in our divorce to where there were rules created in mediation about when a parent could drop items off at the other parent's home. Let your child know you understand this is not easy, but you will do your best to make sure they have what they need in each home. Although I hold my sons to high standards of responsibility, this is an area where I felt I needed to offer grace. It was difficult to manage all the normal "stuff" (backpacks, homework, sports equipment), a child or teen has to and also manage making sure you had the right things in the right home at the right time.

Fourthly, children may feel an extra burden to help their parents manage responsibilities. Of course, children should have age-appropriate chores and expectations, but overall, they need to know you are in charge and can handle managing the home. Because of expectations put on him, I would tell my oldest often, "I am in charge and I will take care of things." Quite honestly, I do not know if I always believed it myself, but I knew God had us and in that I could be confident.

Finally, it is okay to talk about both homes. No walking on eggshells. We had no rules about hiding anything that occurred in our home from their dad. This can make you feel vulnerable, but remember, it is your child who is feeling the pressure of integrating two different worlds. It was okay for them to tell me the fun things they did at their dad's without feeling "sorry" for me. And vice versa, they could share anything that occurred in our home while at their dad's home.

For some children, they may harbor the hope that their parents will reunite. I did not experience this with my children being so young. My eldest's fear was that I would not be there when he woke up in the morning. If you do have this issue, address it gently—although it happens, it is rare and usually once court papers are signed, divorce is final. Your child is grieving as well; help them move through the stages of grief of which denial is one.

Children also need to know that life is not always easy, even for children, but God is with them. Most of all, they need to know that you love them and God loves them more.

God's Priority of Children

And he took the children in his arms, placed
his hands on them and blessed them.
Mark 10:16 NIV

A children's pastor who walked with us through some rough times would often remind me that God loves my children even more than I do. That is hard to comprehend, but He does. I would say to my boys and now my daughter, "I love you so much, but who loves you more?" We may sing "Jesus Loves Me" to our children, but we need to reiterate just how much God thinks of them and cares about them. Children hold a special place in God's heart.

Let's look at Mark 10. The chapter opens with Jesus's teaching I referred to in the first section of the book when Jesus is questioned about divorce. Guess what follows? The next section in the gospel of Mark goes right into Jesus blessing the little children. Did Jesus know children would be the ones so impacted by divorce? Here is the exact wording:

And they were bringing children to Him so that
He would touch them; but the disciples rebuked
them. But when Jesus saw this, He was indignant
and said to them, "Allow the children to co me to
Me; do not forbid them, for the kingdom of God

belongs to such as these. Truly I say to you, whoever does not receive the kingdom of God like a child will not enter it at all." And He took them in His arms and began blessing them, laying His hands on them. (Mark 10:13–16 NIV)

Did you hear that? Jesus was indignant that the children were forbidden. Some versions say "irate" or "angry." Jesus was a defender of children. He spoke up for them as the opening verse of the chapter in this book calls us to do. If children are so important to Jesus, they should be to us as well.

Jesus was a defender of children.

God has consistently called children to Him. Review some of these Old Testament stories with your children.

- Samuel, serving in the temple, was called by the Lord when he was twelve years old (1 Samuel 3).
- God chose David over his older brothers when he was between ten and fifteen years old (1 Samuel 16).
- A little servant girl taken captive from Israel plays a role in Naaman's healing by telling Naaman's wife of Elisha. This little girl had great faith (2 Kings 5).
- The story of King Josiah who became king at the age of eight and, as he grew, had more godly wisdom than adults around him is also meaningful (2 Kings 22–23).

Moving to the New Testament, in addition to the text where the children sit on Jesus's lap, we continue to see God's priority of children.

- Children are some of the first people to recognize and celebrate who Jesus is. We find the use of the word *indignant* again interestingly enough, but this time, it is the religious leaders using it.

But when the chief priests and the teachers of the law saw the wonderful things he did and the children shouting in the temple courts, "Hosanna to the Son of David," they were indignant. "Do you hear what these children are saying?" they asked him. "Yes," replied Jesus, "have you never read, 'From the lips of children and infants you, Lord, have called forth your praise'?" (Matthew 21:15–16 NASB)

Jesus is quoting a fulfillment of Old Testament scripture and children have a role in the fulfillment.

- Then there is the story in Luke 2:39–52 of Jesus at the age of twelve in the temple speaking with the religious leaders. His parents found Him in the temple, "sitting in the midst of the teachers, both listening to them and asking them questions." In my opinion, we can speak God's Word to our children without completely watering it down; they are very capable of understanding more than we give them credit for.
- The story of Timothy has special significance. Timothy had an unbelieving father, but he was taught from a young age by his mother and grandmother the scriptures. A singular parent's faith can have an impact on their child and the world! Give your child a little history about Timothy if it is relevant and share this verse from 1 Timothy 4:12 (NASB): "Let no one look down on your youthfulness, but *rather* in speech, conduct, love, faith, *and* purity, show yourself an example of those who believe."

Finally, often skimmed over is the importance of the little boy with the basket of loaves and fish contained in John 6:1–15. I am including a segment from an article on Paul Tripp's website titled "Don't Forget about The Boy."

One of the reasons I started this "Stories of Faith" series was to focus on the minor and seemingly insignificant characters in Scripture. Whenever we learn about the feeding of the five thousand, we typically hear about Jesus, the crowd, or the disciples, but we neglect this central character. His story teaches us so much.

No one in the crowd would have thought that this boy mattered. No one would have imagined that what he was carrying in his little basket would not only be the provision of the moment, but the basis of one of the most significant sermons Jesus ever preached.

This was one little boy in the crowd, with a little bit of seafood and bread, but he had been chosen by God to be a significant piece of the Messiah's redemptive plan not only for that day, but for the rest of human history.

No one knew that after this moment, every man, woman, and child who trusted in Jesus and read the Bible would know this boy, know exactly what was in his basket that day, and know how Jesus used him to make the point of points about his identity.

Here's what I'm trying to say: **we will never know which little person God will use, and how.** That means that we're never just lost in the crowd. We're never without anything to offer. We never know who the Lord will claim and use in ways that we can't predict, or haven't intended.

The Lord knows us all. He knows where we are, what we have, and how we can be used. He is the Divine Author over each and every moment, writing our stories. He can do eternally amazing

things with the little fragments of our lives that
we're carrying around and that we tend to think
aren't worth much.

This example leads us well into the next section. (And just
remember, children's Bible stories can offer our hearts encouragement too!) Our children need to have a vision; God has a plan for
their lives.

God Cares and Has a Plan for Their Lives

Where there is no vision, people are
unrestrained, But happy is he who keeps the law.
Proverbs 29:18 NASB

Children need to know that God planned for them from the
time of conception and has future plans for them. Share the verse
from Psalm 139:13–16 (NASB):

For You created my innermost parts;
You wove me in my mother's womb.
I will give thanks to You, because I am awesomely
and wonderfully made;
Wonderful are Your works,
And my soul knows it very well.
My frame was not hidden from You
When I was made in secret,
And skillfully formed in the depths of the earth;
Your eyes have seen my formless substance;
And in Your book were written
All the days that were ordained for me,
When as yet there was not one of them.

Children need to know that God is interested in the details of
their life. The Bible tells us that God knows us so well that even to

the point of the number of hairs on our head. He is interested in their hobbies, activities, school, friends, and emotions.

Children need to know God created emotions. When your child's heart is broken, Jesus's heart is broken with them. It is important to help our children process their emotions. Often, when one of my sons was angry, after everything had calmed down, we would discuss the difference between the surface emotion that just occurred and what was really bothering them underneath the anger. Anger is often a cover emotion for other more vulnerable emotions. Pray with your child for wisdom in interpreting their emotions. God knows our thoughts before we speak them. Something we do with our daughter now is give her a simplified feeling wheel. I am amazed at the accuracy of the emotion she is feeling when she is able to point to it on the chart. She would not have been able to voice it with words. (If you are not familiar with a feeling wheel, they are great for adults and children! At the end of the book, under "Recommendations," there are links for the simplified version and one more appropriate for teenagers.) Remind your child that emotion, even anger, is not sin. It is what we do with our emotions at times that is sin, not the emotion itself.

Refrain from telling your child the emotion that they are feeling. In this case, the little words you use count. Using words like *appear* or *seem* or *wondering* gives your child a voice to verify their feelings. For young children, you can express and give them words such as "You appear to be really angry." Even calling attention to how you came to this conclusion, such as your arms are crossed and your face is scrunched. I give you a more lighthearted example to practice this with. Parents often say things like "We had fun today." Something more appropriate would be "I had a lot of fun today. How was it for you?" You can take it a step further and ask, "What was the best thing we did today? What was not as much fun for you?" This may seem trivial, but you are giving your child the ability to express themselves appropriately and this will take them far in life and relationships.

Children need to know who they are in Christ because the rest of the world as they knew it has changed. Quoting again from Marquardt:

Growing up in two worlds creates endless and often painful complications for a child. But the first and most troubling consequence is that resembling a parent is no longer the mark of being an insider, a part of a large family to which the child and other family members belong. Quite the opposite. Suddenly, resembling a parent, or sharing any kind of experience with a parent, can also mark the child as an outsider.

Children need to know that God is their ultimate Father. When they feel confused about family, they need to know first and foremost that they are a child of God. One of my most precious memories I have is when my adopted daughter and I were out for a bike ride, and she unabashedly was singing out "I Am a Child of God." It is from the Bethel song that I had sung to her at night. Music is powerful for children too. Here is a portion of the song.

> From my mother's womb
> You have chosen me
> Love has called my name
> I've been born again
> Into Your family
> Your blood flows through my veins
> I'm no longer a slave to fear
> I am a child of God
> I'm no longer a slave to fear
> I am a child of God

Although our girl was adopted, I draw parallels in how she had apprehensions on resembling or having memories of her other foster families and her biological home. We had to make it "okay" and encourage her to share her memories, but mostly, we wanted her to know she was adopted by her heavenly Father. (By the way, isn't God so good in how He prepares us for situations we have no idea are coming? There are many circumstances I have dealt with in our divorced situation that prepared me for parenting our girl through foster and adoption.)

If you have any type of tapestry or cross stitch in your home, use it as an example of life. Show your child the beautiful front and finished picture, and then show them the back. All the threads knotted can look like rather a mess, but the artist knew what they were doing in creating something beautiful when finished. Share this verse from Ephesians 2:10 (NLT), "For we are God's masterpiece. He has created us anew in Christ Jesus, so we can do the good things he planned for us long ago."

Another visual example is that of the potter and clay. The skilled potter takes a lump of clay that one cannot see the beauty in and makes a beautiful vessel.

> But now, Lord, You are our Father; We are the clay, and You our potter, And all of us are the work of Your hand. (Isaiah 64:8 NASB)

Applications
Chapter 4: Your Children

1. Remember to open up conversations, but be careful to let your child express their feelings. Using words like *appear* or questions as "How is this for you?" Use a feeling wheel. Do not take their feelings personally. Be in the frame of mind they need you to enter into their story.

2. Ask your child what their feelings are regarding the divorce? Sometimes it helps to have them draw a picture. What is the hardest part of having divorced parents? Are there any positives? My sons may have said at their dad's they get to play video games. However, while accepting this graciously, I was also not going to change my parenting style.

3. What is your child having to navigate right now? What are they grieving?

4. What are they worried about? Although we cannot and should not do everything for our children, how can we help? Calendars, text reminders, calming strategies, etc.

5. How do they feel God feels about them? Share with your child how important children are to God.

SINGLE PARENTING

And now a word to you parents. Don't keep on scolding and
nagging your children, making them angry and resentful.
Rather, bring them up with the loving discipline the Lord
himself approves, with suggestions and godly advice.
—Ephesians 6:4 TLB

Changing Parental Roles

When you see the Covenant-Chest of God,
your God, carried by the Levitical priests,
start moving. Follow it. Make sure you
keep a proper distance between you and it,
about half a mile—be sure now to keep your
distance!—and you'll see clearly the route to
take. You've never been on this road before.
Joshua 3:1–4 MSG

As a single parent, you will navigate new roads just as the
Israelites did; you have never been on this road before. Read the first
few chapters of Joshua to get the context of the above verse. Moses
has passed, and God is giving instructions and encouragement to
Joshua as he takes over leadership. In best case circumstances, children will still have contact with a dad and mom. However, it will not

be in the same house at the same time. Therefore, your role as parent will change whatever the circumstances or custody arrangements. Sometimes, it will feel like you need to be all things for your child at once. Is it exhausting? Absolutely, but also joyous in its own right. God will grow you up in areas that you thought you were weak in. There were probably things you relied on your spouse for because he/she was better at it or it was just the roles you had fallen into.

I often felt like I had to be a mom and dad at the same time. I had a kind, gentle voice, and when necessary, what I called my "dad voice." I was the nurturer and at the same time the disciplinarian. I had to cook dinner and play catch outside. I had to do the budget and read bedtime stories. I had to mow the lawn and clean the bathroom.

I was now the spiritual leader and role model of our home as well. I strongly believe we, as parents, first and foremost, need to be teaching our children at home both directly and indirectly by our example about God's ways. This is the parents' job, and the church's job is to support our efforts.

Sometimes, when our children go through pain, we feel like we should go easy on them. However, your child will be looking to you for stability. They will look at you, and possibly test you, to see if you will enforce boundaries. Boundaries do make children feel secure and loved. You can understand their pain and still keep expectations. Remember that life is often holding two things in balance. You are helping balance your child's world for them.

It is helpful to read parenting books so you do not feel alone in your parenting. I would often read and reread the *Strong Willed Child* by Dr. Dobson. Sometimes, all I needed was the reassurance that I was doing it right and to hang in there. I always had the mind frame that I could learn something more from a new perspective about biblical parenting. If there was a parenting class at church, I would join if the timeframe worked for me. Is it hard to attend a parenting class as a single? Yes, it was, but my focus was on being the parent God called me to be in my unique circumstances.

You are never too old to discover new parenting concepts as times change. I am still learning as we parent our daughter! Sometimes even gleaning one piece of advice helps. Following is a brief overview of some things I learned that may be a helpful place to begin on your single-parenting journey. I list parenting books for different age levels in the back of the book. My goal was to read at least one new parenting book a year. If you are more of a listener than a reader, tune into *Focus on the Family* or *Family Life* (see "Recommendations"). A side warning: Just make sure to pick the days when they are talking about parenting and not marriage! The especially hard episodes on these talk show platforms for me are when they discussed marriages on the brink of divorce that pulled through, and I would wonder why God did not save my marriage. Then I would have to remind myself…this was God's plan for my life and I do not have to compare my life with others.

Raising Men and Women of Character

> May our sons in their youth
> be like plants that grow up strong.
> May our daughters be like stately columns
> which adorn the corners of a palace.
> Psalm 144:12 GNT

As a parent, it is vital we have an end goal in mind. We are not just raising boys and girls. We are really raising men and women. I loved the early stages of childhood and have such fond memories of when the boys were young. However, I always had in mind that I did not want my children to stay in childhood. I desired for them to grow into godly men who could lead a family, have a career, and make wise choices for themselves. Everything we learn in childhood builds on making us into who we are as adults. One of the most helpful books I read was *Raising a Modern-Day Knight: A Father's Role in Guiding His Son to Authentic Manhood*. It gave me a vision of the men I desired to raise. Yes, I do know that the book was written for fathers, but as you try to understand your children, feel free to pick up books that are intended for the role you are not in! That goes for the books I list in recommendations at the back of this book.

The definition for *manhood* in *Raising a Modern-Day Knight* is "real men reject passivity, accept responsibility, lead courageously, and expect the greater reward." I wrote this vision of manhood in my prayer journal and prayed I would be able to nurture those things in my young boys. I also wrote the "code of conduct" given in the book which is a "a work to do, a woman to love, and a willingness to obey" and prayed for these as well.

At times, I felt a little out of touch as a mom relating to other moms. Other moms cried at fifth-grade promotion, and I was just excited to see my sons growing and entering a new stage in life. Even when my oldest left for college, there was definitely sadness and adjustment to living life without him in the house. At the same time, I was proud that he was able to make decisions and branch out on his own. Did I agree with all his decisions? Absolutely not. Was it hard to watch and know when to intervene and when to let him learn on his own? Absolutely! Parenting does not end, but it does change. However, there are now ways I am seeing the fruits of labor, and parenting may some days feel like "labor"! Garrett, now at age twenty-one, as I write this, will be graduating and has already accepted a job. He is planning on taking over his medical insurance, car insurance, phone bill, and all those things adults need to do. I do see him rejecting passivity, accepting responsibility, and leading courageously. I am continually praying that Garrett recognizes how God has watched over him.

I also see these fruits in my younger son who had a difficult decision to make concerning college. He was sought after by colleges to play football. However, he had a lifelong goal in mind. What would the purpose of playing in college be and what would happen after college? Would he get any more concussions that would affect the rest of his life? He made what I think is the more mature adult decision against what many others and our culture thought he should do. The scripture that his dad and I had chosen to be read at his dedication when he was still an infant is "Be on the alert, stand firm in the faith, act like men, be strong. All that you do must be done in love" (1 Corinthians 16:13–14).

I thank God that even at a young age, Nate could make wise decisions for his own life. There were many times I observed adults around him making poor decisions, and yet Nate stood strong. His high school football coach said of him in a newspaper article: "Great player, better person." Character will take you further in life than sports or academic accomplishments.

I prayed for my sons to grow like Jesus grew. "And Jesus grew in wisdom and stature, and in favor with God and man" (Luke 2:52 NIV). The Jews were looking for a king that would take over with force and conquest, but Jesus was distinctive because of his character. Jesus used His power in humility and for good of those around him. Proverbs 22:1 (NASB) reads, "A good name is to be more desired than great wealth, Favor is better than silver and gold." Proverb 22 is the same proverb that contains the much-quoted verse, "Train up a child in the way he should go." So as your children grow, keep the end goal in mind and that is raising them to be able one day take on responsibilities and decisions of a grown up. It starts now. One way to do this is to concentrate on character. Of course we look no further than the Bible to find those character traits we want to instill in our children that will help them be successful adults. Two scriptural references come to mind:

> But the fruit of the Spirit is love, joy, peace, patience, kindness, goodness, faithfulness, gentleness, self-control; against such things there is no law. Galatians 5:22–23 NASB

> Now for this very reason also, applying all diligence, in your faith supply moral excellence, and in *your* moral excellence, knowledge, and in *your* knowledge, self-control, and in *your* self-control, perseverance, and in *your* perseverance, godliness, and in *your* godliness, brotherly kindness, and in *your* brotherly kindness, love. For if these *qualities* are yours and are increasing, they do not make you useless nor unproductive in the true knowledge of our Lord Jesus Christ. 2 Peter 1:5–8 NASB

Drawing from the lists above, when you praise your children, point out the character trait they are displaying. This does take practice and mindful parenting. It is easy to say "good job," but try to take that a step further and point out the trait you see the most in the action your child took. My sons excelled in some sports, and I told them I was proud of those accomplishments. At the same time, I emphasized more the traits they displayed. For example, for my son who did cross-country, I would point out the perseverance it took to train and finish a race. Those are qualities he can apply to other areas in life for the long term. I will cover a few traits here, but you will know the traits your child demonstrates and those they need to work on.

During their high school sports years, we were the family that gave rides to all the kids on the teams who needed them because my sons looked out for others. We anonymously paid an athletic fee for a teammate because my son was concerned the teammate would not be able to participate. During COVID, when my son was doing school at home, he had a friend who was required to do in-person school. Nate was not going into school himself during COVID. However, when that friend needed a ride, Nate would get up early and bring him. When I saw them being kind to each other as brothers, it blessed my heart. (Believe me, with two boys, there was a high level of competition in our house as well which was maybe why I latched on to those times of kindness!) I would point out they were demonstrating "kindness" to others around them. Those things made me more proud than winning races or football games. We live in a culture where no one "loses" anymore, and everyone is awarded for just being on the team. Trophies mean little because everyone gets one. I recall one time everyone on my son's baseball team received a trophy. My son did not play much in this particular tournament, and he recognized on his own that he did not "earn" the trophy. He actually destroyed it! I do not commend that action (see self-control below!), but it should wake us up to the reality that deep down, even children know when genuine praise is deserved.

Another trait to concentrate on is self-control. Notably, science has found that the trait of "self-control" in young children determines how successful as adults they will be. Here is a quote from American Scientist,

> To our own surprise, our 40-year study of 1,000 children revealed that childhood self-control strongly predicts adult success, in people of high or low intelligence, in rich or poor, and does so throughout the entire population, with a step change in health, wealth, and social success at every level of self-control.

Of course, the Bible is way ahead of science! Note that self-control is listed in each scripture above. Every time your child says "no" to the influences around them, they are demonstrating self-control. This is something we can instill in them from a young age. There are probably more times than you will ever know about when as teenagers that they have to say "no" to going along with the crowd, so make sure you find those times as youngsters and give ample praise!

Perseverance is a quality that is needed in every area of life from learning a new skill to our human relationships. The Bible says if perseverance is increasing, it will make one useful and productive. Hand in hand with this is teaching, our children will need to deal with disappointments in life. Sometimes, the things children are disappointed about may seem trivial to us, but this is a prime opportunity to help your child voice a feeling and take action if needed. From our own adult experiences, one thing we know is life will hold disappointments. Rather than attempting to completely protect our children from disappointments, we need to teach them how to approach, deal with, and overcome disappointments. Proverbs 24:16 (NLT) says, "The godly may trip seven times, but they will get up again. But one disaster is enough to overthrow the wicked."

Another noteworthy trait is patience. I point this one out because I call this the "Amazon" age. We may be tempted to give our children everything they want immediately. I really did not have to deal with this with my sons. With my daughter, she expects things to be immediate and delivered to the doorstep the next day! This is what I mean when I say I am still learning about parenting because parenting sometimes changes with the times. One night after a family walk or "roll" through the neighborhood, my daughter stepped on her skateboard, and it broke in two pieces. Immediately, she said, "Let's just get another one." Well, her skateboard is a good thing; it gets her exercise and energy out, but we did not like the attitude behind the request. There was no waiting, no patience! It is our job as parents to help her develop that trait. This was the perfect situation to have her save up some money, and we took our time getting a new skateboard.

This is the prime time to practice our patience as well! Remember even we are continually working on the fruit of the spirit in our lives. Be patient with your child. Why did God relate these characteristics to fruit? It was something people in the day could understand, and maybe if you have fruit trees, you can relate in a more personal way. Fruit does not just appear. Some fruit trees may not even bear fruit for the first five years or more! Even in one season, many things have to happen for the fruit to become edible—pollination, fertilization, growth and development, and finally, ripening. As we invest time into our children, be patient with the growth. Know the work you are putting in matters.

As we invest time into our children, be patient with the growth. Know the work you are putting in matters.

Furthermore, keep in mind that one of the best ways to teach our child is by our example. We also need to cultivate these traits in our lives and be honest about where our struggles lie—which traits are more difficult for us. Your kids know anyway! Just how much our children learn from our example was reiterated to me by our daughter just the other day. We had just finished putting all the groceries in the car, and she had taken on the job of putting the cart into the return rack. Well, I turn around, and all of the sudden, I see her with multiple carts pushing toward them toward the return. When she got back to me, I asked, "What were you doing with those other carts?" She said they were just sitting in the parking lot.

"What made you want to put them away too?" I asked, and she said, "Mom, that is what you would have done." Woah, that was a good thing for her to emulate, but what about the times I am impatient or not grateful?

Finally, when thinking about raising children who will one day need to be competent adults, we need to begin to teach our children to make wise choices. Give them practice now. They can begin to make small choices. As they grow, they make more important choices—like how many hours can I work and still do well in school? Although my sons knew I was the ultimate decision maker, I often asked their opinions on topics that affected the whole family.

I remember a time my son had to make a decision about continuing guitar lessons. Together, we listed the pros and cons, and for the time being, he was the one who decided to keep taking lessons. Translating that to adulthood, Garrett had three job offers on the table. Because he learned to process decisions, he had the competency to think it through and pick the best offer for him. Keeping that end goal in sight, we are moving on to more of the nitty gritty of parenting.

Power of Prevention

Prepare your work outside,
And make it ready for yourself in the field;
Afterward, then, build your house.
Proverbs 24:27 NASB

Setting up a home environment that eliminates problems in the first place will save you time and energy. Sleep is so huge and overlooked. You may be surprised at how much sleep is recommended for different ages. I included sleep guidelines in the appendix. I quote this from the *Journal of Clinical Sleep Medicine*.

- Sleeping the number of recommended hours on a regular basis is associated with better health outcomes including: improved attention, behavior, learning, memory, emotional regulation, quality of life, and mental and physical health.

- Regularly sleeping fewer than the number of recommended hours is associated with attention, behavior, and learning problems. Insufficient sleep also increases the risk of accidents, injuries, hypertension, obesity, diabetes, and depression. Insufficient sleep in teenagers is associated with increased risk of self-harm, suicidal thoughts, and suicide attempts.

Even with adequate sleep, down time is good. When they were past the napping stage, I still required my children to have a daily down time if we were home. Often we would do it together and make it another reading time. Often I would be the one to fall asleep! Obviously, this was based on the day of the week and activities going on, but it is a good habit to have with your children. It teaches them to self-monitor as they grow older, to give themselves breaks when they need it.

Daily physical activity also helps our brain and impulse control. As a teacher, I was highly discouraged as districts cut recesses in favor of more academic time over the last twenty years. Three recesses became two recesses until, eventually, there was only one lunch recess. In many districts, gym time is minimal as well. That said, do not count on your child getting their physical activity level met at school. Taking a walk or bike ride after dinner is good for the whole family. Involving your child in a sport or physical activity at the right age is positive as well. Just keep in mind, in America, we tend to overschedule our kids so keep balance in mind. We did one sport a season.

Eating well is a huge passion of mine. For my sons and our adopted daughter, I truly believe we have eliminated behavior problems by watching what we eat in our home. At suppertime, they ate what was made, or they did not eat. I was often criticized for our strict eating habits; we had no corn syrup, no food dyes, and no gluten in our home. We mostly used natural sugars. If we could afford it, we ate organic food but didn't obsess over it. We just ate real food—mostly meat and veggies. You would think this would be a positive thing, but I often got negative push back from others. However, I have to say that my sons as adults have developed very healthy eating habits. On their own, they have determined what foods make their bodies feel healthy and which do not. To me, I have given them a lifelong gift. Refer back to the opening scripture, though, keep a half mile between you and the ark or the goal in sight; you do not have to rush new things, you can incorporate them slowly.

Limit tech use for brain health. Handing your child a device is so easy. Parenting is a long road, and when we use easy solutions, they become detours. We set ourselves up for back-tracking, which makes for a longer, harder journey. (I think most of your parenting of teens is actually done in the toddler years!)

Parenting is a long road, and when we use easy solutions, they become detours.

My sons each had half an hour of computer time; it was the only device we had. My daughter now has the same amount of time on the computer. My sons never had television time unless it was a VHS video; my daughter now has one hour a day. Sometimes I think even this is too much. If we see an attitude change, we are quick to note how characters are behaving even in her kid shows.

Timers are our best friend! There is no arguing about when a show or game was started. Children can be taught to set their own timers, just another way you are teaching your child to begin to self-monitor. I do have to note after the timer rang, we would reset it for a final five minutes. This gave their brains time to know it was time to end and finish up anything quickly.

However, if I could do one thing differently in parenting, I think it would relate to phones. I am grateful the boys did not have phones until they turned thirteen. Delay this as long as you can. My son's dad insisted on buying their phones and setting up their accounts. I paid half the monthly fee. However, I had no control over their phones. My husband and I attempted to put a safety device on the phones, but we were constantly disconnected. Their dad had no screening on their phones. This is something I should have pushed back on harder. This is a battle I should have fought. I would have paid the entire monthly fee to know that certain content was being blocked. Never in parenting has there been this issue of handing your child a small device that has so much possibility for evil as it does for good.

We did have the rule no phones in the bedroom at night. My oldest had that rule through high school, and somehow, we got more lackadaisical with our second son. He is the one who has called me out on that. Overall, in parenting, I felt like I parented both sons together at the same time, with the same rules. If I could go back, I would take into account their age differences and individualize parenting more based on their age. So learn from my mistakes, it will take more energy to individualize but keep your eye on the end result. I am not a tech person, and I cannot cover this new area of parenting with any kind of expertise. Please buy and read *The Boogeyman Exists and He's in Your Child's Back Pocket*. Technology has some upsides, but we need to have a healthy fear of the dangers that lurk on the internet and social media. In fact, buy a copy for your ex too. This is a battle to fight if need be.

One more note, no computers in the bedrooms ever. Always keep your computer out in an open area. With that said, there was one issue I disagreed with in some of the parenting books I read. One or two books recommended letting your child keep their room in a manner they desire and shut the door if you do not like it. From my perspective, messy rooms do affect the whole house because dust spreads (I am a bit of a cleaning fanatic!). Teaching your child how their actions impact the rest of the house is important.

However, more importantly, closed doors shut your child off from the rest of the household. It tends to make them more secretive. In my opinion, the symbol of a closed door gives the impression you do not desire to be involved in their life. We had an open-door policy. Rooms had to be reasonably cleaned and picked up. They definitely were allowed to but, rarely, went into their room and closed the door. This could be my children's personalities. I was so fortunate that they often chose the common space to hang out and that would just open conversations we otherwise would not have had. When we had outgrown our blessed 850-square-foot home, my husband and I looked for a new home with an open concept for communication purposes. I feel so fortunate that my children still opt to sit in the open area rather than locked in their rooms.

Keep in mind you only have control in your home environment. It would be best for your child if you can communicate with the other parent. For me, this was not the case, and I had to concentrate on what happened in our home. At one point, my sons were getting negative stickers at their dad's. I was not sure where this concept came from, but I had no control over it. However, I was able to counter that with lots of praise in our home.

Parenting Guidelines

Correct your son, and he will give you
comfort; He will also delight your soul.
Proverbs 29:17 NASB

The following are some helpful techniques I learned that helped me to parent alone on a day-to-day basis.

Make your expectations known

First, another preventive measure, let your child know expectations before you go to church, the grocery store, a friend's home, etc. Every time we were in the car, I would talk about what we were going to do and what was expected of them. Sometimes there were new situations where I did not know what to expect, and I would prepare my children for that as well. Do not inundate your child with rules because they will stop listening. A few clear guidelines usually suffice. Also, let them know the consequences if the guidelines are not followed.

That leads us to few words usually have more impact. Do not give long lectures to your child, especially during a crisis or a time of high emotion. I learned that boys respond to short, simple commands and consequences delivered calmly. During times of crisis, their brains are not ready for instruction so your words are wasted anyway! I would then pray that during other times, situations would arise where I could address the issues I needed to. The Bible says to talk about God and his ways all the time. "These words, which I am commanding you today, shall be in your heart. And you shall repeat them diligently to your sons and speak of them when you sit in your house, when you walk on the road, when you lie down, and when you get up" (Deuteronomy 6:6–7 NASB).

Be prepared for transitions

In general, transitions are hard for most children. As a teacher, my lesson plans included how we would transition from one activity to another because I knew this is where most behavior problems would occur. Children in divorced homes have more transitions to manage. Just think about it: They could have two homes, school and possibly childcare or after-school care, all of which have a different set of standards. Transitions were hard; I would verbally remind the boys, "Hey, you are at Mom's house now and remember what our rules are here." Please do this without criticizing the other parent's home. Yes, how the other parent manages their home can have an impact on our lives, which I agree is frustrating. However, most of the time, there is little we can do, but we can teach our children how to switch gears. I found that there were things I could do to ease the transitions. For a while, I played the same praise song whenever my sons came home. Think sensory; have a pleasant essential oil smell in your home like lavender. We all use the same lavender- or vanilla-scented homemade hand lotion in our house. An uncluttered, welcoming environment can help as well. My sons and I often sat for ten minutes, and I gave them my eye contact and undivided attention when they returned from their dad's home. Making those connections would ease us into our time together.

Consistency and consequences

The number one word in parenting to me is *consistency*. It will be tiring, but we are following the example of God as our constant.

So let's not allow ourselves to get fatigued doing good. At the right time we will harvest a good crop if we don't give up, or quit. Right now, therefore, every time we get the chance, let us work for the benefit of all, starting with the people closest to us in the community of faith. (Galatians 6:9–10 MSG)

I mentioned before when we take the easy way out, we backtrack in parenting and take the longer detour. The time invested up front may seem wasted but we have the long-term picture in sight. One example I give is the following: I expected my boys to behave in the grocery store. I would carry Nate in the pack in front of me, and Garrett would sit in the cart. Well, one day, Garrett was in a mood, trying to get out, and I had already given him a warning. I left my cart (felt a little guilty for this but probably saved other shoppers from an unpleasant experience!), picked Garrett up, and walked out. We went back home and had to return later in the day. Did this mess up my day? Yes, it was a fifteen-minute drive to the store so we wasted time, but guess what? Never again did I have to do that. Garrett loves food to this day and is an excellent cook, so food was probably the motivation! But can you see how sacrificing the one day translated into many happy trips to the grocery store? Stay the course; do not be tempted by the detours.

Consistency across all environments is crucial. There was a time I overheard my son talking rudely to his stepmother at a baseball game. I was rather surprised by this as he typically was polite to adults. And there was a part of me that sensed some gleeful retribution. In the end, my adult brain won out. I wanted my son to be respectful to all adults, and I corrected him and had him apologize.

Using consequences wisely will improve your parenting outcome. Never ever give a consequence you are not willing to follow through on. For example, "I am going to take away all your toys" or "You are grounded for a month." I just did this. My daughter poured a glass of almond milk and did not drink it. I told her more than once to put it away and save it for later, of which she did not. I then dumped out the milk and said she could not have milk for a week. Oops, I think a week might have been a little too long, but I said it and my goal is for her to trust my word, so I will need to follow through. It is okay to say you need to think over the consequences and you will get back to your child. Two things are essential to note: You are teaching your child they can trust you; they can trust your word. You keep your promises. This is so crucial! Secondly, you are preparing them for the real world. The real world has consequences.

If possible, the consequence should match the situation. A natural consequence, for example, is when the boys did not stop their computer time when the timer rang, then the next day, they did not have their time. That was an easy one, but all parenting is not so cut and dry. This is why it is a good idea to think and pray or even talk about it with a wise friend before exacting a consequence. Natural consequences, however, are not always possible. There were many times that I would take away a toy even if it did not relate to the situation at hand. My sons made it easy. They memorized all their matchbox cars, and I could take away one, and this would be upsetting to them. Obviously, the takeaway changed with the age of the boys.

Once you get good at natural consequences, your child can sometimes make their own consequences! I found my sons were sometimes better at thinking of natural consequences than me. One day, my youngest son decided it would be humorous to shake up his Zevia soda and squirt all over his brother in the kitchen. As I was mulling over what consequences to give him for messing up his brother, the kitchen, and wasting his drink, the boys on their own said, "Nate probably should be grounded from Zevia." How wise and simple! (And yes behind their backs, I smiled. I did understand the thought process of a boy sneaking up on his brother for a surprise attack.) Another time, my oldest in his teen years was getting in a pattern of being unkind to his younger brother. I talked to him about where his attitudes were coming from, and he grounded himself from an app on his phone for two weeks. Of course, he may have been concerned that the take away I thought of would be worse!

It is also okay to have grace at times, give a warning, and the consequences that will occur if the action is repeated. If the action is repeated, follow through. However, do not count! This may be a personal pet peeve of mine, but I learned through my many years of teaching that all counting accomplishes is to teach children they do not have to listen right away; they can wait for the arbitrary number you have chosen.

Use your authority well

Parenting strategies are not secrets! In the end, we want our children to learn how to parent when they grow up. I would often share with my boys why I needed to correct a certain behavior and that I had an end goal in sight. I also deferred to the authority who created my children. I would explain that one day I would stand before God, and I would be responsible for my parenting decisions. God was my ultimate authority.

I would explain that one day I would stand before God, and I would be responsible for my parenting decisions. God was my ultimate authority.

However, next to God, you are the authority in your home. Do not give away your authority! Never threaten your child with an authority that is fictional such as Santa. (I have my own opinions on Santa. I could never lie to my children about this but would ask them what they thought. It comes back to once again we want our children to trust our word.) I also once overheard a parent say that they had the police come to their home to talk to their young children. Who do you want your children to respect? If you are handing your authority over to others, your child, as they grow, will learn you are not the authority they need to listen to. This is detrimental in teen years, and it will ultimately damage the relationship they have with you.

If you do get remarried one day, I recommend you continue to manage the discipline. If your children are young, a stepparent may be able to over the course of a few years ease into this role, but it should be taken very slowly. I was so fortunate to have had many years to establish my relationship with my children. When I remarried, my husband's role was as a mentor to my children. I maintained all discipline. I would consult him in private about decisions to be made, but I was the one who followed through on those decisions. For our family and the age of my children at the time, this eased a lot of tension that occurs in stepfamilies. (Blending families is difficult enough!)

Power of Routines and the Power of Flexibility

There is a time for everything, and a season
for every activity under the heavens.
Ecclesiastes 3:1 NIV

Many people imagine that the hardest time for children of divorce is the moment when their parents first part. That moment is hard, but it is only the beginning. The division and restructuring of childhood that immediately follow, and which continue up to and beyond the point the child leaves the home, throw into question aspects of childhood that were once taken for granted and keep the divorce very much alive for years to come. (*Between Two Worlds*)

As I stated before, routines can help alleviate a lot of behavior problems. They create a security for a child whose life has often been turned upside down. If there were bedtime routines that you had before you were divorced, then keep those same routines if at all possible. This will be a comfort to your child. The teacher in me asks that you include reading as part of that routine! I believe in reading to even your older children. If you have children of varying ages, try to find a book that will appeal to all to make it easier on yourself. If possible, keeping routines the same at both households helps as well. Although never communicated, I believe the boys' dad continued the same bedtime routine we had begun.

Another routine that is important is dinnertime. Somehow, even after my ex-husband had left the home, I managed to sit down each night with my three-year-old and baby for dinner even if it was for ten minutes. To this day, sitting down to dinner as a family is a priority. As children get older, schedules will conflict, but do your best to have dinner together. It is a great time to reconvene after the day. Share your thoughts; the easiest for all ages is to share the best thing, and the worst thing about your day. We also at different times used family conversation starter cards.

Flexibility is key as well. There were times I desired to embark on a family adventure that I could tell my kids were not emotionally and physically up to when they returned from their dads. Was I upset that they were worn out and now I had to postpone what fun activities I had planned? Yes, but remember to keep your children's needs in focus. (Refer back to John 21!) Sometimes what they needed was just some good down time. When you understand and meet that need, the bond they have with you increases.

Sometimes, all the neighborhood kids were out playing, and I let them stay out a little later. When you have developed overall consistency over a period of time, it becomes easier to tweak a rule now and again. I felt fortunate in some ways that my children were so young, and I could lay the foundation of how our home was to be. If your children are older at the time of divorce, more habits will have already been formed. Dramatic changes may not be your best option. Referring back to the verse in the beginning of chapter 5, remember to keep the ark (your vision for your home and parenting) in sight, but keep a half mile as you and your child journey on this new path.

Teaching Safety

I looked for someone among them who
would build up the wall and stand before me
in the gap on behalf of the land so I would
not have to destroy it, but I found no one.
Ezekiel 22:30 NIV

When I think about parenting, I think that we are often in the position of "priesthood." Priesthood means we stand in the gap for our children when they are young. It means we look for those places where there are holes in the wall of protection we build around them. I think for children in divorced homes, those gaps tend to be larger. We need to start from the assumption that in our home, we will cover all the topics that relate to safety.

You are the educator to teach your child general safety such as staying home alone, internet safety, fire safety, as well as sensitive topics such as what are the private parts of your body, and sex education. Unless you have a clear understanding with your ex of what you and they will teach, the job falls on you as head of your current household. Obviously, I had boys so I could not relate to the physical changes that occurred for them, but I purchased the *Focus on the Family Design for Sex* books and went through with my sons. There are materials to help discuss topics that may make you feel uncomfortable, so do not avoid these topics or think your child will learn these things elsewhere. This is your responsibility. Check the resources at the back of the book for additional materials.

Asking for Forgiveness and Accountability

Brothers and sisters, even if a person is caught
in any wrongdoing, you who are spiritual
are to restore such a person in a spirit of
gentleness; each one looking to yourself,
so that you are not tempted as well.
Galatians 6:1

You have a lot of demands placed on you and you will not do it perfectly. One of the best pieces of parenting advice I received was, it is so beneficial to ask your child for forgiveness when you mess up. In fact, in that simple act of humbling yourself, there is so much learning that occurs on both sides! There is so much deepening of the relationship.

First, your child learns how to go to another person, admit a fault, and ask for forgiveness. Parents learn that children are the best role models for us when it comes to forgiving! My sons were always quick to forgive me and move on. They also would ask for forgiveness when they have spoken to me rudely. Often, when a rebellious teen emerged, within the hour, they would come to me and ask for forgiveness without me saying a word.

Secondly, children realize they do not have to be perfect. They are more open to coming to you with the truth when they do mess up. They are more apt to go to God when they sin. They have given grace and experienced grace.

Just know that if you have not been in this practice of seeking forgiveness, it is never too late. Even when my sons were adults, I felt prompted by the Holy Spirit to write them a letter confessing some mistakes I made as a parent. I am so glad I listened to the prompting because afterward, one of my sons was able to talk about one of his struggles in life.

Along these same lines of giving and receiving forgiveness, accountability to each other is biblical in community but truly starts with the family community. My children to this day are some of the best people who keep me accountable. One of my sons is the first to recognize if I am going in a negative direction when talking about others (aka gossip) and calls me on it. I appreciate the reminder. When the boys were young, one of my pet peeves was name-calling. There is a difference between giving someone a label like "whiner" and just pointing out that, at the moment, they might be whining. Children carry labels with them into adulthood. As a family, we decided we would all hold each other accountable for "name-calling" and that included me. I messed up the other day with my daughter and called her "sassy girl." She immediately pointed it out. Guess what? She was right, and I immediately apologized. Much more appropriate would be that your tone at the moment is sassy. Overall, she is a pleasant child, and I never want her to grow up thinking she is "sassy."

Obviously, if you give your children permission to hold you accountable, they need to do it in a loving and respectful way as well. Share the verse, "Brothers *and sisters*, even if a person is caught in any wrongdoing, you who are spiritual are to restore such a person in a spirit of gentleness; *each one* looking to yourself, so that you are not tempted as well" (Galatians 6:1 NASB).

Children's Activities

She keeps an eye on everyone in her household,
and keeps them all busy and productive.
Proverbs 31 MSG

We need to find the right balance for our children's schedules, not enough activity and futility can set in. Too much activity and we are asking for behavior problems and overload. Each child is different in this area. One of my son's is definitely an introvert, and it helped me tremendously to read *The Hidden Gifts of the Introverted Child* by Marti Olsen Lainey. (Note: This is not a Christian book; check it out from the library.) This is the time to explore and find out what each individual child's skills and talents lie as well.

However, this is tough because if children are to be involved in activities, both parents almost always have to be on the same page. My children experienced stress over the different priorities their dad and I had. I wish it could have been different for them.

Music was important to me because I think it helps brain development. Both boys took guitar but only on my time. This made it difficult to be consistent. I am glad they each had the opportunity, but it was something I had to let go because of circumstances. It was not worth the battle. My country music–loving son now wishes he would have kept it up!

Their dad and I both saw the benefits of sports, but I was adamant that it not consume our lives. Traveling sports was something I had to take a stand on, and it was addressed in mediation. In my opinion, traveling sports are a family commitment, and that often means siblings have to sacrifice. Sometimes it means that families are divided when they could be spending time together. I realize this is not popular public opinion in America. Let me give a few reasons why I take this stance. I do not think that our worlds should center around a child's schedule. What that teaches a child is exactly that, life should center around them—not something we as Christians desire to teach our children. Furthermore, variety in sports and activities shape a more well-rounded adult, both physically and emotionally. Fortunately, the mediator was able to resolve these issues. I use my sons as perfect examples that you can excel at sports in high school and reap the benefits without sacrificing your family. That being said, if travel sports or activities were already part of your life, you may need to continue just to keep consistency for your children.

From a young age, both boys knew that they would need to get a job that worked with their school schedule when they turned sixteen. This is not something their dad exactly supported, but also not something he opposed. This did fall on me to enforce.

Church activities, although important, are also something you will have to work through. If both parents are on the same page, that is helpful. My sons did Awanas until upper elementary because it fell on my time. I had decisions to make once the youth group age hit. It would mean giving up valuable family time. Every other Sunday was the only consistent time for family night, so youth group was something we forewent. I still have mixed feelings on this decision, but I did take seriously that I was the one to train the boys up in the way they should go, and I know God honors that. I felt like giving that time up would mean losing time we spent together as a family in the Word and prayer. More on this to follow.

Hunting was something my youngest son desired to do with my husband. Nate was passionate about this, and his dad had major concerns about hunting. This was another issue we were fortunate enough to work out in mediation. Nathan now is an avid outdoorsman and will hopefully build his career on this passion.

Look for your child's passions and build on those. Work with your ex if you can on developing and building on each child's individual talents. Much has been taken away from your child, but building on talents God has instilled in them brings meaning and purpose.

Applications
Chapter 5: Single Parenting

1. Read Joshua 1 and take encouragement as God is with you as you take over leadership of your family.

2. Be honest: What are your parenting strengths? What are your parenting weaknesses? Be intentional about getting help where your weaknesses lie. If it is discipline, read books or listen to podcasts on biblical parenting. If it is organization, read or listen to tips on how to organize your home or calendar. While I am a great planner and organizer, I am aware of one of my weaknesses slowing down to savor a moment.

3. Visualize the kind of adults you would like your children to become. What values and characteristics would you like them to have? Some character traits come easy for our children. Some children are naturally compassionate. I often think it is the traits that come harder for our children that we need to concentrate and develop in them.

4. What family decisions can you let your child contribute to?

5. How much sleep is your child getting? Does it meet the requirements listed in the back of the book? Would any of your children benefit from "down time"?

6. How much physical activity is the family getting on a daily basis? We live in Wisconsin, so I know this is hard in a cold climate, but bundle up and get outside! I am fifty, and my husband is fifty-five, and we still sled with our daughter. Recently, we took up cross-country skiing. Movement is good!

7. What new healthy eating habits can you incorporate? Start small if you need to.

8. Technology: how is it used in your home? Is there conflict about how it is used between the two homes? Read *The Boogeyman Exists; And He's In Your Child's Back Pocket: (FIRST EDITION) Internet Safety Tips for Keeping Your Children Safe Online, Smartphone Safety, Social Media Safety, and Gaming Safety*. Do not delay.

9. What are transitions like for your children? How can you ease transitions? Think sensory—music, eye contact, etc.

10. Do you need to ask your child to forgive you for any offense?

REBUILDING YOUR FAMILY

Again I will build you and you shall be rebuilt,
O virgin of Israel!
Again you shall take up your tambourines,
And go forth to the dances of the merrymakers
Jeremiah 31:4 NASB

There is hope for your family! God is in the business of rebuilding lives and healing broken hearts. As the pieces fall in place, you will feel like a family again. The routines you put in place will help with this. Some family traditions may come to an end, but you will start new ones. You will build memories that your child will carry with them throughout life.

While I was looking for a new home, the boys and I moved in with my parents. God provided a blessed house for us. We called it our "little green house." This was the perfect time to have our family picture taken to grace the walls of our new home. It was a step in rebuilding our family unit and visualizing that "we are still a family."

At the introduction of this book, I confessed how I attempted making life decisions without including God. I thought I was doing things "right," building my life, but I was not consulting God in all parts of that building process. The idea of rebuilding with God is exemplified in the book of Haggai. For greater understanding, read the entire book. It is only two chapters long! Obviously, they were rebuilding the temple, but let us apply the concepts to rebuilding our lives with God as our foundation.

Let's break it down and see how it applies to our lives as we seek to rebuild our families. Haggai is a minor prophet who was sent to call the people to repent and rebuild the temple. The book of Haggai comes at a time when the original, magnificent temple Solomon had built had been destroyed. Haggai is calling on the people to rebuild the temple. At the time, the people were only concerned about their own homes as testified to in Haggai 1:3–4 (MSG), "How is it that it's the 'right time' for you to live in your fine new homes while the Home, God's Temple, is in ruins?" The *Moody Bible Commentary* says Haggai was rebuking the people for their "inverted priorities." It states they "disobeyed God with their inverted priorities." Sadly, this reminds me of myself many years ago—using the materials God had given me to build my own life rather than thinking about building the "temple" where God dwells.

Take a connection leap with me. Obviously, the people were rebuilding a physical building, but are we not God's temple? See 1 Corinthians 6:19 (NIV): "Do you not know that your bodies are temples of the Holy Spirit, who is in you, whom you have received from God?" Build your temple, your life, with Him as the foundation. God allowed hardships to come to the people of Haggai's time, but the good news is the governor, the high priest, and all the remnant of the people took "immediate and dramatic corrective" action. In response to their obedience, God encourages them along the way. He reassures them in Chapter 1 verse 13, "I am with you." Take hope, my friend, God is with you as you seek to "rebuild." You are not alone.

As it goes, the supplies for the temple have been collected, plans made, but as the rebuilding begins, discouragement sets in. First of all, the people were rebuilding amongst a ruined city. Can you relate? Do you feel like you must begin to rebuild amongst devasta-

As we rebuild, we need to reframe our vision for our family (renewed perspective) as well as hear God's encouragement for those times that discouragement will threaten to take over.

tion? Secondly, those that had seen the original temple were disappointed in the simplicity of the new temple and they could not help comparing. This temple seemed so inferior. Beginning in chapter 2, God gives His people renewed perspective and encourages them three times (according to *The Moody Bible Commentary*, thoughts also taken from *What the Bible Is All About: Bible Handbook*). As we rebuild, we need to reframe our vision for our family (renewed perspective) as well as hear God's encouragement for those times that discouragement will threaten to take over.

First of all, I love that in chapter 2 verses 3–4, God acknowledges how they must be feeling discouraged. See the questions asked from God through Haggai in verse 3. "Who of you is left who saw this house in its former glory? How does it look to you now? Does it not seem to you like nothing?" Three questions are followed by three encouragement commands. Haggai tells them three times to "take courage" or "be strong" and continue the work. Are you feeling discouraged? God knows, God acknowledges your feelings and He is saying to you "take courage" and "persist and persevere in working."

Secondly, God reminds them again that, as in the past, when He brought them out of Egypt, His presence is still with them here and now. Verse 5 says, "My spirit remains in your midst. Do not fear!" (NASB). His Holy Spirit is actually in us! Reread 1 Corinthians 6:19 above.

The third encouragement looks to the future: God would take an inferior temple and fill it with His glory. In fact, it states the latter glory will be greater than the former and "in this place I shall give peace." Now we know that God's ultimate peace and glory come in future eternal life. This life will still have trials, but I believe God gives us glimpses. Read all of Psalm 27, and be encouraged by the last two verses.

> I would have despaired unless I had believed that
> I would see the goodness of the Lord
> In the land of the living.
> Wait for the Lord;
> Be strong and let your heart take courage;

Yes, wait for the Lord.
Psalm 27:13–14 NASB 1995

Armed with renewed perspective, ready to persist in the task of rebuilding, let's look at some practical ways of doing this.

Peaceful Abode

The fruit of that righteousness will be peace;
its effect will be quietness and
confidence forever.
My people will live peaceful dwelling place,
In secure homes, in undisturbed places of rest.
Isaiah 32:17–18 NIV

I could never compete with all the luxuries my sons' dad provided, but I was able to make our home a peaceful place to live. In reality, it is not the physical building or the size of the building that makes a home a home. It is your foundation that begins on God that provides the security for your home. I absolutely love the following verse and visualized and prayed that our home would be a fortress where my children could find peace and bring emotion, a safe place where they could be themselves and find protection for their souls.

"Whoever fears the Lord has a secure fortress, and for their children it will be a refuge" (Proverbs 14:26 NIV).

Do you see? It did not begin with a building, it began with me as the leader of the home having my heart right with God, fearing God. Your home begins with you as you make God your foundation.

The Message version of the Bible says, "The Fear-of-God builds up confidence, and makes a world safe for you children" (Proverbs 14:26 MSG).

The Proverb directly after that says, "The Fear-of-God is a spring of living water so you won't go off drinking from poisoned wells" (Proverb 14:27 MSG).

These are principles we lean into, not promises that our children will never rebel or drink from "poisoned wells." That said, having a peaceful home draws children in. Feeling God's love surrounds them like a sweet aroma draws them in. "But thanks be to God, who always leads us in triumph in Christ, and through us reveals the fragrance of the knowledge of Him in every place" (1 Corinthians 2:14 NASB).

Although it starts inside us, that peace should translate to our outside world as well. I do believe in the order of a home. It is hard to feel peace inside when our physical outside world is chaotic. God does commend order. "But all things must be done properly and in an orderly way" (1 Corinthians 14:40 NASB). This was written for the church order, but the first example of church for our children should be our homes. The first example of living in a community should be experienced in our homes.

A Word on Holidays

Sing to the Lord, all you godly ones!
Praise his holy name.
For his anger lasts only a moment,
but his favor lasts a lifetime!
Weeping may last through the night,
but joy comes with the morning.
Psalm 30:4–5 NLT

I come from an Italian family on my mom's side. Holidays were so important. Food that accompanied the holidays was even more important. On Christmas Eve, it was traditional fish and fresh *curdidi*. On Christmas Day, it was Italian beef and lasagna. Frittata—a most excellent egg dish with multiple cheeses and sausage—we ate the night before Easter. And who would think about having the Fourth of July without a pasta dish? Well, for us, every holiday had a pasta dish! So finding out many years ago I had a gluten allergy and felt my best eating a paleo, grain-free diet meant I had to reframe holidays; they were not just about food!

When time is divided between parents, precious holiday time is split as well. You need to reframe; holidays do not always have to occur on a specific date to be important or to create memories. You can also create new family traditions. Santa can come any day. Actually, my sons knew from a young age that Santa did not exist. As I mentioned before, I struggle with the concept of asking your child to trust you and yet lying to them about a fictitious character. You can use your own judgment. We did not have money for a lot of presents, so aka "Santa" Mom just filled their stockings with things like figs and Italian nougat candy.

My sons would come home from their dad's Christmas Day and be tired of opening presents for hours. If we truly wanted to enjoy our opening time, scheduling it for another day worked better. Again, it was not in the day, it was in the time we spent together. My extended family was gracious enough to attempt to accommodate our ever-changing schedule. Frittata night changed to any weekend before Easter that worked with our schedule.

A new tradition we began as an immediate family was decorating the tree together sometime around Thanksgiving. We would have cocoa, turn on Christmas music, and get to work making the house festive. We also began a "sleep by the Christmas tree" night too. I honestly do not remember how this began, but sometime between the setting up of the tree and Christmas, we threw blankets on the floor and went to sleep by the light of the Christmas lights.

Another tradition we began was on Valentine's Day. I think Valentine's Day is a great day to tell the people in your life that you appreciate them. It does not have to be just about romantic relationships. Everyone in the family got a card with their name on it. Each family member wrote some kind things on it about that person. It was a positive experience that we continued for many years and still do with whoever is at home at that time. We also had a New Year's Eve dinner, celebrated with wine glasses filled with fake wine, and it was not always on New Year's Eve. It was just a way to welcome in the year as a family.

Take care of yourself around the holidays as well. I knew Christmas time was going to be hard for me when the boys were not home, so I planned ahead for it. I often went on a winter hike at a park or made sure I had some good books to read. Do what you need to, to pamper yourself a little and ease the sadness that can accompany the holiday time. Also, review your feelings that emerge around holidays. What were they like growing up for you? Are there better and new memories you would like to instill in your family? Both my husband and my dad come from alcoholic homes. For them, lots of feelings emerge at this time and not always positive. Holidays did not always bring back good memories. As I encouraged you earlier in the book, take this time to work on yourself and heal past wounds so you are a healthier person and parent.

Family Night

Go, therefore, and make disciples of all
the nations, baptizing them in the name
of the Father and the Son and the Holy
Spirit, teaching them to follow all that I
commanded you; and behold, I am with
you always, to the end of the age.
Matthew 28:19–20 NASB

We had an excellent children's pastor who emphasized parents and the home were the first teachers of the gospel. The church's role was to support what the family was doing at home. With those thoughts in mind, when both boys were young, we began family night and continued family night through high school. It was a struggle at times, especially as the boys got older, with the divided time they spent at both homes and other outside activities. However, I believe it was worth the effort.

Do not be deceived; these times did not go perfectly. Sometimes the boys were rolling around on the floor wrestling or began doing these little instigator behaviors kids do. That said, I also did not approach this time rigidly. They could lay or fidget with something as long as they were mostly attentive. It was an informal, relaxed time. There is a time for everything—a time to be more formal in our worship and come to God with fear and trembling and a time to sit at His feet like Mary and learn from him.

Our time included a short devotional, prayer, and a game. We kept a family prayer journal; we wrote down the date and our prayer requests. We often looked back to see how God answered prayer and wrote down praises. I let the boys write their requests. Again we were very informal, some of the entries I look back on include "more ice cream" and one that warms my heart from my football player son who does not appreciate hugs anymore! He wrote "more hugs from mom and Garrett." Some requests were, of course, more serious. We passed the journal and took turns praying. We just talked to God; we did not close our eyes. Sometimes I think I may have messed up. Should we have been more reverent? I am not sure, but I do want my children to see God as accessible, as a friend. Looking back at my journals, I recorded that Nate gave his heart to God and it was during a family night. It was actually during a time I was struggling with was my life having any impact on others. Discipleship starts at home. God encouraged my weary heart and the angels in heaven celebrated over one sinner who repented.

It is also important to have fun as a family. Game time gave the boys something to look forward to, and of course, there was usually some kind of food treat too. The boys took turns choosing the game we would play.

We also did family movie night on occasions. We would rent a movie, lay out blankets, and eat popcorn in the living room. Typically I did not allow eating in the living room so this was something special.

Your family traditions will look different than ours, but put some time into thinking about how this could look for your family. Sometimes you try something and it doesn't click, try something else. Traditions can bond your family and provide connectiveness. Give your children input, what are these things they would like to begin or continue? My husband was a little surprised by how many times my boys would say to him, "Well, that is our tradition." Until he pointed this out, I did not even realize how much stock the boys put into those traditions.

Church

So let's do it—full of belief, confident
that we're presentable inside and out. Let's
keep a firm grip on the promises that keep
us going. He always keeps his word.
Let's see how inventive we can be in encouraging
love and helping out, not avoiding worshiping
together as some do but spurring each other on,
especially as we see the big Day approaching.
Hebrews 10:22–25 MSG

Make going together to church as a family a priority. Depending on your situation, you may have to choose a new church. I know it is hard to do on your own, but gather your courage because it is important you show your children God still is the center of your life. If you do stay at the same church, I pray you have people who come alongside you. You still may wonder what others think or say about you. There is only one fear that is appropriate and that is the fear of God, not of man.

I sometimes felt like an anomaly—all these happy intact families around me. It stood out to me in church more than in other environments. In reality, all families have some kind of brokenness or struggle even if from the outside they look perfect. I could not join married couples Sunday school, but I joined the parenting ones when I could. I am grateful to those that came alongside me and supported me in my parenting journey. The wife of our youth pastor at the time came from a divorced home and reached out and had us over for monthly dinners.

Sometimes, I felt a heaviness about going to join other families at events at church, but it was then more than ever that I knew I had to break through. Remember the spirit of discouragement does not come from God. Ephesians tells us where it does come from, it is a spiritual battle, a scheme of the devil:

Put on the full armor of God, so that you can
take your stand against the devil's schemes. For

> our struggle is not against flesh and blood, but
> against the rulers, against the authorities, against
> the powers of this dark world and against the
> spiritual forces of evil in the heavenly realms.
> Therefore put on the full armor of God, so that
> when the day of evil comes, you may be able
> to stand your ground, and after you have done
> everything, to stand. (Ephesians 6:11–13 NIV)

Like Joshua, know when you lead your family, you do not go alone. Joshua 1:9 says, "Have I not commanded you? Be strong and courageous. Do not be afraid; do not be discouraged, for the Lord your God will be with you wherever you go." And say as Joshua did "as for me and my family we will serve the Lord."

Giving to Others

> A generous person will prosper; whoever
> refreshes others will be refreshed.
> Proverbs 11:25 NIV

There are points in life when we feel all consumed by our own lives. This is understandable. Ask God to bring small ways that you can reach out to others. This will lift your spirit and is an example to our children.

Although we were on a tight budget in our home, my boys had everything they needed and more. I wanted them to know that most of the world does not live the way Americans do. I chose a World Vision child between the ages of both boys, and together, we would pray for him on family night and talk about how his life is different from ours. My daughter now has a Compassion International girl around her age. I had my oldest son volunteer stocking shelves in a food pantry one summer. We filled shoeboxes as a family for Samaritan's Purse. We sent money anonymously to a single mom. These may not seem like huge ventures, but it is important to take your eyes off your circumstances at times and think of others in whatever small ways you have the energy to reach out.

When I got remarried, we looked for further ways our family could reach out to others. We became a Big Family to a grade-school boy. It was tough. We did our best to provide some experiences for him he would not otherwise have received. He played on a flag football team with the boys. We did family meals with him. In the end, his family moved to another state. The experience left us feeling like it was really hard to have an impact on his life and behavior for those very short times. That is when we began to consider fostering. It was a family decision because it would affect everyone in the family. Our daughter ended up being the only child we fostered. She needed a lot of one-on-one time in the beginning, but we know she was meant to be with us. My sons were very much a part of being her big brothers and spending time with her. She has enriched each of our lives. And it was my youngest son who pointed out once Savannah was adopted, what was the next mission for our family? It reminds me of a verse from Romans 15:3–6 excerpt: "God wants the combination of his steady, constant calling and warm, personal counsel in Scripture to come to characterize us, keeping us alert for whatever he will do next."

I also resonate with the verse in Zechariah 4:10 concerning the rebuilding of the temple. It says, "Do not despise this small beginning, for the eyes of the Lord rejoice to see the work begin, to see the plumb line in the hand of Zerubbabel. For these seven lamps represent the eyes of the Lord that see everywhere around the world" (TLB). From my limited understanding of carpentry, a plumb line runs vertically and is used for measuring straight lines. When we stay connected vertically to God as our source, He will provide the direction for us and the little acts of faith grow. Of course, it is not by our power, as it says earlier in chapter 4 of Zechariah, "Not by might, nor by power, but by my Spirit, says the Lord Almighty—you will succeed because of my Spirit, though you are few and weak." Anything we do for others is offered up as a sacrifice to God because He is the One who gives us the strength to do it.

Vacations

So on the seventh day, having finished his task,
God ceased from this work he had been doing.
Genesis 2:2 TLB

Family vacations are an optimal time to bond, but again, divorce can make things complicated. Depending on your custody schedule, you may have to plan ahead. We had two vacations per year if we desired to take more days than our custody time allotted, and we had to enter it into a Family Wizard schedule and the other parent had to approve it. Not fun, but necessary. As the boys aged, their dad decided two vacations per parent was too much time away from sports, and we were down to one extended vacation per year.

Again, you can reframe vacation, especially when money is tight or children are young. However, make sure to schedule in days for relaxation. It can make life seem normal again. When the boys were very young, I just did some staycations. A day at the beach with a picnic lunch can be a refresher. Touring your own town or one close by can be interesting as well. We did a yearly family vacation with extended family. However, as the boys grew, I decided to pursue what originally their dad and I thought we would raise them, to be lovers of nature, and what better way than to go camping. I had been camping since I was a young girl, and their dad and I had camped at Yellowstone and the Smokies in addition to Wisconsin's beautiful state parks.

My eldest was six, and my youngest was three. This was the year to try. I had all my parents' old camping equipment and began to get excited as I pulled it out. I also thought of the obstacles of camping as a single mom. If one of us had to go to the bathroom, we all had to go (thank goodness I had boys!) And what about showering? I would have to take them with me. Some people advised me to join another family or a camping group, but I felt confident that this needed to be our family's time together, a bonding just for us.

I talked to the boys about the things we would do and cook and about my memories from childhood. I picked a smaller state park that I felt I could navigate easily. The big day had almost arrived, and the night before my youngest came home from his dad's with a case of poison ivy. I expected him to get that in the woods, not in someone's backyard! At least, I had a homeopathic poison ivy remedy packed. Should we still go? A call to the doctor confirmed poison ivy and the nurse told me to put calamine lotion on it. The next morning, Nate had more patches, but he was bright-eyed and ready for adventure.

We got to the campsite early. If you tent camp, you know the first thing you do when reaching your site is establish the most level spot for the tent. This campsite had a tree in the middle, so there really was only one place to put the tent. Within two hours, I have everything ready—the tent and screen tent up, the clothesline hung. This would be our "home" for the next few days. With plenty of time, we checked out the beach and took showers. We built a fire, and I started to relax. An older woman came and told us what a great job we were doing and how it reminded her of when she would camp with just her son out under the stars in California as a single mom. I consider this a God thing—a sign of his encouragement and goodness. I was going to need it!

We sat down to roast our traditional first night of camping dinner—hot dogs—and Nate is not hungry. Unusual. He wants to go to bed. Highly unusual. He felt warm. For my extensive medical kit, I took out the thermometer. His fever was 101. Do not ask me why I packed a thermometer and not something to bring down a fever. It was getting toward dusk. These were the days when cell phones were still new; I had an old borrowed one that was not getting reception. Between the rash and the fever, I decided we need to go get this checked out. We were in the middle of farm country; the two closest towns had populations of less than two thousand. We raced to the nearest small town seeing signs for a hospital. This also in the days where there was no "Google maps." I was reading a paper map. We got to the hospital and we were directed to a clinic. We were the last patient they took that night and only because we were camping.

The nurse asked me if we needed a prescription, where would I have it sent? I have no idea! She kept asking even after I explained our situation. I felt badgered, and tears welled up in my eyes. Thank goodness the doctor came in, and she was so kind. After checking Nate out, she reassured me that the rash and fever are unrelated. Just give him Motrin. She drew me a map to the grocery store and also how to get back to the state park. God bless her. (This is a reminder, we never know when we are kind to people how much it can mean! The nurse took my confidence and the kind doctor gave it back.) We got back to the campsite. The fire was dying down and so was my adrenaline. Garrett asked, "Will we still make smores?"

"Tomorrow, if we stay."

Nate, feverish and almost asleep, yelled out, "We have to stay!"

We crawl in the tent and under the covers and are asleep in minutes. I am awakened by something brushing against the side of the tent. Should I turn on the lantern to scare it? Just a racoon, I am sure. We have many racoon stories from camping as a child. Exhausted, I go back to sleep.

The next morning, I arise as the boys continue to sleep. I got the camp stove ready. This is the old kind you actually have to pump to get the fuel into the burners. I take my first sip of coffee made in a percolator. There is nothing like that first sip of coffee when you are out in the woods. The boys woke up and Nate looked better.

"Are we staying?" they asked me.

"Yes, we will try." We ate breakfast—bacon, eggs, cantaloupe, and pineapple cake with cream-cheese frosting. The boys start playing. I cleaned up—boiling water to do the dishes in the same tubs my mom used almost thirty years ago. We spent the day, much like I remember as a child—hiking, lunch, swimming, showers, playing catch, supper, and a campfire. That night, I again heard the brushing sound on the outside of the tent near my head. I calmed my overactive imagination and went back to sleep.

After hiking the next day, I went to grab something from the tent. I saw a hole in the tarp (by the way, if you want to stay dry, tarps should always go on the inside of your tent, not underneath!) and under the tarp was a hole in the floor of the tent. My first thought is, *What a cheap tent! Maybe a rock ripped the bottom?* I looked back in the hole and I saw what I thought were baby animals curled up in a hole in the ground. Should we just take down the tent and go home?

Instead we went to get the ranger. He removed the babies into a box and duct-taped our tent floor. (Duct tape is now on my list of essentials to bring camping.) Are they mice? No, he says they're too big for mice. Will the mom come back? The ranger said he did not think so. I searched the whole tent and our luggage for any sign of an animal. That night I lined the whole side of our tent with heavy objects, afraid the mom may try to return even though the ranger says she will not. He stopped by the next morning to check on us and told us it was actually a cottontail rabbit's babies.

"I thought you said the mom would not return."

He chuckled and said, "Well, I had hoped not." This helpful ranger is another sign of God's goodness.

So as it turns out, the grassy spot where I set up the tent must have had a nest burrowed in the ground, and the mom came back at night trying to save the babies. I felt really bad, but I also felt a kindred spirit with the mother rabbit. The same fierce spirit is instilled in me when it comes to doing the best for my boys. That mother rabbit did what she did due to natural instinct. We do what we do because we have the cognizant knowledge that our children are a gift from God placed in our care.

One may think I never want to venture a solo camping trip again. However, I felt empowered, even with all the obstacles, we did it. Garrett saw his first indigo bunting; he kept a list. Nathan caught grasshoppers camouflaged to look like pieces of grass. They both collected hickory nuts and learned to watch out for the invasive species, white parsnip. We played football at the lake. We roasted marshmallows and read *Magic Treehouse* by the fire. We went to a nature show and learned about snakes in Wisconsin. Our last walk around the campsite, and Garrett started picking out campsites he would like for next year. Hooked! By the way, does Coleman's warranty cover a rabbit chewing a hole through your brand-new tent? The duct tape lasted for years by the way, and we continued doing yearly camping trips the boys consider some of their best memories. Nathan, as I mentioned previously, became a true nature lover and would prefer being outside than being inside!

The boys, together, did a backpack trip in Shenandoah recently. When your children are gone on an adventure like that, even if they are grown, you have to trust God to take care of them. More recently, Nate went kayak fishing the other night, in the middle of the night to be exact. This is when you catch catfish. I was encouraging him to go and excited for him. Then I was getting ready for bed and realized Nate was out there all by himself, in the middle of the lake in the pitch-black darkness. I wondered why I so readily encouraged him. I think one of the reasons is, I have lots of practice placing my kids in God's hands because many times, I had little control over where they were or what they were doing.

Applications
Chapter 6: Rebuilding Your Family

1. Make a vision for the kind of home you would like to create for your children. Is your home a refuge for your children? Ask your child what kind of home they envision. Write down all their ideas and make a family mission statement.

2. What are holidays like? How can you reframe? What are new traditions?

3. Would a family night work for your family? What would that look like? Involve your children in planning.

4. Who can you reach out to? Is there a ministry or volunteer opportunity you could participate in as a family?

5. If you cannot afford vacation, what kind of staycations can you do?

7

PRAYER: YOUR MOST POWERFUL TOOL

Prayer is a tool that is made mostly of words,
but it's no less a tool than one made of steel.
—Eugene Peterson

As a parent, especially when our children are young, we expect to basically know what they are doing, who they are with, and even what they are eating. Divorce changes all of this. We often send our children off, and we do not have much knowledge of what occurs in the other home. We do not get to choose who our child is spending time with or even who is babysitting them. However, having less control means giving God control, but it does not mean we remain inactive. We may feel powerless, but we have a weapon that is sharper than any two-edged sword, God's Word, and we can pray God's Word over our children. We can cover them in prayer.

> *However, having less control means giving God control, but it does not mean we remain inactive.*

I recommend the book *Every Child Needs a Praying Mom*. My eldest son saw this book and said "Every child needs a praying dad too." He is so right; so, Dads, here is a venue for you. I tell my son maybe he can write that book when he grows up if no one beats him to it. To this day, I do not think there is a book with that exact title.

So as difficult as it may seem, daily heed Paul's advice from Philippians 4:6–7 (MSG) and I mean daily because it may seem like a daily battle.

> Don't fret or worry. Instead of worrying, pray. Let petitions and praises shape your worries into prayers, letting God know your concerns. Before you know it, a sense of God's wholeness, everything coming together for good will come and settle you down. It's wonderful what happens when Christ displaces worry at the center of your life.

Sometimes prayers are answered; sometimes, we wait for what seems like an eternity. Sometimes God answers differently, and sometimes God has a sense of humor when He answers. I will share a short, humorous story with you. I will start by saying I know there is not necessarily a right or wrong answer to this situation. However, it was not in my repertoire to take my children on vacation and then leave them in a "kids club" with adults they do not know. The boys' dad was going on vacation to a resort and planning to put the boys in the "kids club." I was completely against this; the boys had enough change, adjusting to a new person living in their dad's house. There was nothing I could do. I requested he leave them at home, but that was not going to be an option. So they went and I prayed. When the boys got home, I asked them how the kids club was. Their response was they did not attend. The day they were to be dropped off, there was some kind of masquerade holiday, and the workers were dressed up. The masks scared the boys. Read Isaiah 40 to discover the God who made the intricacies of the earth is in control, not any human. God shows me this again and again.

In the following section, I will share with you the scripture prayers I prayed for my sons often inserting their name right in the passages. This will get you started, but your children will have their own unique needs. I have a spiral notebook with each family member's name sticking out on a sticky note, not fancy at all! After their name, I leave many pages that I fill with scripture prayers for them.

God will give you the right prayers at the right time for each of your children.

So pick up your tool and begin praying!

I began to pray 2 Thessalonians 2:16–3:5 (NIV):

> Lord, may You Yourself, our God and Father who loves _______and by Your grace gives _______ eternal encouragement and good hope, encourage his/her heart and strengthen him/her in every good deed and word.
> Lord, may he/she be delivered from wicked and evil men for not everyone has faith.
> But, God, You are faithful.
> Strengthen and protect _______from the evil one.
> May _______ continue to do the things he/she have learned from Your Word
> May You, Lord direct ___________heart into Your Love and Christ's perseverance.

Notice the verses mention strengthening and protecting. In the case of praying for my children, God put it on my heart to pray they were strengthened inwardly (soul and spirit) and to pray they were protected outwardly. Lastly, that the teachings and Word of God they have learned would cause spiritual growth in their lives.

Inner Strength

Here are some of the inner strength verses I prayed for my sons. I prayed my sons would have a spirit like Caleb. Numbers 14:24 (NIV) says, "But because my servant Caleb has a different spirit and follows me wholeheartedly, I will bring him into the land he went to, and his descendants will inherit it." When the rest of the world is saying "yes," more than ever now, our children need to be able to stand up and not fear being different, even going against the majority as Caleb did.

In that line of thought, I prayed these two verses as well,

> For the Spirit God gave ____ does not make him/
> her timid, but gives him/her power, love and
> self-discipline.
> 2 Timothy 1:7 NIV

> May ______ not be conformed to this world, but
> be transformed by the renewing of his/her mind,
> so that ____ may approve what the will of God
> is, that which is good and acceptable and perfect.
> Romans 12:2 NASB

I prayed the following verses for their minds not only to be renewed, but protected and governed by the spirit.

> The mind governed by the flesh is death, but the
> mind governed by the Spirit is life and peace.
> Romans 8:6 NIV

> And the peace of God, which transcends all
> understanding, will guard your hearts and your
> minds in Christ Jesus.
> Philippians 4:7 NIV

I would also pray that their spirits would convict them of wrong, and if they were not convicted, they would get caught if they made poor choices (aka sin). Quite honestly, we also need to pray this over our own lives as well.

> The spirit of a person is the lamp of the Lord,
> Searching all the innermost parts of his being.
> Proverbs 20:27 NASB

I do have a story regarding this prayer. When my oldest went away to college, he did get involved in some of the world's ways. He purchased fake IDs. I knew he had them, and I actually prayed about it and then left it in God's hands. A few years later and quite near his twenty-first birthday, he was Doordashing and pulled down a street that was closed due to construction to deliver his order. A police officer stopped him, and as Garrett was pulling out his license, he saw a fake one and confiscated it. I smile at the story because God is faithful and good. He hears our prayers and answers in His timing.

Obviously, we pray for our children to see God's goodness and faithfulness as well, not just his discipline. Again my oldest was away at college and had not paid his parking spot fee. The company technically had stopped billing him for a few months but eventually caught the error. The manager called him, and Garrett told them he would be there in twenty minutes, although he knew he did not have the money to pay. He called me and said, "Mom, what should I do?"

I answered what every good mom should answer, "Do the right thing. Be a man of your word and go to their office."

So Garrett heads to the office and tells the manager that he will pay whatever he has on his debit card. His card had been compromised recently, and he had put a hold on it a few days before. Although the card should have worked by then, it did not. Now the amazing part was, whether out of frustration or sympathy, the manager waived the fees and let Garrett off the hook. God is faithful. That was not a coincidence; it was God showing up when Garrett chose to do the right thing.

Outward Protection

I have to tell you, there is a verse in the Bible that specifically applies to children of divorce who go between two homes. Of course, this may have not been the psalmist's intention, but check out the following verse. Psalm 121:3–8 (NIV) is a great prayer of protection and the ending to me seemed so applicable to my children who were forever "coming and going" between two homes.

> He will not let _____'s foot slip—
> he who watches over _____ will not slumber;

> indeed, he who watches over ______
> will neither slumber nor sleep.
> The Lord watches over ______—
> the Lord is _____'s shade at his/her right hand;
> the sun will not harm ___ by day,
> nor the moon by night.
> The Lord will keep _____ from all harm—
> he will watch over his/her life;
> the Lord will watch over his/her coming and going
> both now and forevermore.

Furthermore, I would pray Deuteronomy 28:6 (NIV) that they would also "be blessed when they come in and blessed when they go out."

Did you know we do not have to be helicopter parents because God is a helicopter God? The God who hovered over the earth and brought all things into creation is the same God who will hover over our children (see Genesis 1:2). The meaning of *hover* is to remain or linger in or near a place. Our God is hovering over our children. He is near them and remains with them when we cannot be.

> He found him in a desert land,
> And in the howling wasteland of a wilderness;
> He encircled him, He cared for him,
> He guarded him as the apple of His eye.
> As an eagle stirs up its nest,
> And hovers over its young,
> He spread His wings, He caught them,
> He carried them on His pinions.
> Deuteronomy 32:10–11 NASB

As I mentioned before, I appreciate word pictures and the Bible uses them eloquently. These verses I could see in my mind's eye, my sons being cared for by their loving Father. Read and study all of Psalm 91, but I especially like verses 11–13 (NIV).

> For he will command his angels concerning you
> to guard you in all your ways;
> they will lift you up in their hands,
> so that you will not strike your foot against a stone.
> You will tread on the lion and the cobra;
> you will trample the great lion and the serpent.

When my second son was still so young, I had to let him go to spend nights at his dad's. This verse brought me comfort as I saw Jesus carrying Nate in His arms.

> He tends his flock like a shepherd:
> He gathers the lambs in his arms
> and carries them close to his heart;
> he gently leads those that have young.
> Isaiah 40:11 NIV

I will end this section with a verse from Psalm 139:5 (NASB): "You have encircled me behind and in front, And placed Your hand upon me." God is hovering above your children, carrying your children, and His angels are holding them up.

Spiritual Growth

> So then neither the one who plants
> nor the one who waters is anything
> but God who causes growth.
> 1 Corinthians 3:7 NASB

At nighttime, I would pray over my boys that God would help them grow healthy in their body, mind, and spirit. As I mentioned before, I would pray that they would grow like Jesus did, "And Jesus grew in wisdom and stature, and in favor with God and man" (Luke 2:52 NIV).

In 1 Chronicles 28:9–10 (NASB), there is an address given to Solomon by his father, David, before the people.

> As for you, my son Solomon, know the God of
> your father,
> and serve Him wholeheartedly and with a willing
> mind;
> for the Lord searches all hearts,
> and understands every intent of the thoughts.
> If you seek Him, He will let you find Him; but
> if you forsake Him, He will reject you forever.
> Consider now, for the Lord has chosen you to
> build a house for the sanctuary;
> be courageous and act.

From these verses, I would pray my children would know God, serve Him with their whole hearts and a willing mind, seek Him, consider Him, and do the work He has for them.

I also prayed that anytime they needed encouragement or conviction, they would remember God's Word.

"But may the Helper, the Holy Spirit, whom the Father will send in My Name, He will teach you all things and bring to remembrance, all that I said to you" (John 14:26 NASB).

And that God's Word would do a work in their lives,

> For the word of God is living and active, and
> sharper than any two-edged sword, even pene-
> trating as far as the division of soul and spirit, of
> both joints and marrow, and able to judge the
> thoughts and intentions of the heart. And there is
> no creature hidden from His sight, but all things
> are open and laid bare to the eyes of Him to
> whom we must answer.
> Hebrews 4:12 NASB

Our prayers are not guaranteed immediate answers. We have to keep in mind that our children will be adults who need to make their own decision for Christ. They cannot rely on our faith. That said when my oldest turned eighteen, although he faithfully attended church not once questioning it, I now left the decision to him. I have seen too many kids who live double lives to please their parents—one in the church and one the world.

We may not see our prayers are answered, but the one comfort I have is once a prayer is prayed, it remains. I may not leave my children a great monetary inheritance, but when I am gone from this earth sitting with Jesus my prayers over them remain.

I may not leave my children a great monetary inheritance, but when I am gone from this earth sitting with Jesus my prayers over them remain.

Prayer for their Sibling Relationships

One thing that struck me is my sons actually ended up spending more time with each other than either parent because they went back and forth together. Therefore, I felt I needed to pray that their bond was healthy and strong and could endure. Nate seemed to find great comfort in the fact that his brother was a constant for him. I prayed the oft used Ecclesiastes 4:9–12 (NIV).

> Two are better than one,
> because they have a good return for their labor:
> If either of them falls down,
> one can help the other up.
> But pity anyone who falls
> and has no one to help them up.
> Also, if two lie down together, they will keep warm.
> But how can one keep warm alone?
> Though one may be overpowered,
> two can defend themselves.
> A cord of three strands is not quickly broken.

Prayers for Friends

One who walks with wise people will be wise,
But a companion of fools will suffer harm.
Proverbs 13:20 NASB

I prayed and continue to pray God would bring good friends into their lives and remove friends that may not be good influences or just not good for our particular child. Prayers for our child's discernment and wise judgment are also needed because they will be the ones who ultimately pick their friends. Keep in mind just because a peer is in church or youth group, we still need to be cautious.

It is my opinion that sometimes our society places too much emphasis, especially with social media, of having many friends. However, it is my desire and prayer that my child has one or two faithful friends rather than a multiple of "friends." I have seen God answer and provide "friend" prayers for a particular season of the boy's life. I have seen God answer by removing friends—often by using the boy's discernment. I have seen God bring a friend that has a similar interest.

I also prayed as I could for their specific friends. I actually have listed many of their friend's names in my prayer journal. I would keep a football roster in my Bible so I could pray for those on my son's team. Although I may have only prayed for them for a season, I know as well those prayers stand.

Prayers for Their Future

I will instruct you and teach you in
the way which you should go; I will
advise you with My eye upon you.
Psalm 32:8

Although issues often seemed urgent and I would place the current situations before God, I also realized that as I stated before, I was raising men. That meant I should spend some time thinking and praying for their future, that meant future careers, future spouses, and future ministry.

Praying for our Son's Futures

Drawing again from *Raising a Modern-Day Knight*, the author writes that the Bible lays out a code of conduct for sons which the book defines as: a will to obey, a work to do, and a woman to love. I will break down how I prayed for each one of those.

Will to obey

First, a will to obey is defined in the book as "God's will as revealed in the scriptures." Second Timothy 3:14–17 (NIV) is a great verse for this concept.

> But as for _____, may he continue in what he has learned and has become convinced of, because he knows those from whom he learned it, and how from infancy _______ has known the Holy Scriptures, which are able to make him wise for salvation through faith in Christ Jesus. All Scripture is God-breathed and is useful for teaching, rebuking, correcting and training in righteousness, so that _________ may be thoroughly equipped for every good work.

Work to do

The above scripture aptly leads us into "a work to do (according to his own unique design)." God has a unique gifting for each of our children. As we watch them grow and experiment with different activities, we should be looking for those things that seem to bring life to them. It is their job in the end to figure this out, but we are there to guide them.

For we are His workmanship, created in Christ
Jesus for good works, which God prepared
beforehand so that we would walk in them.
Ephesians 2:10 NASB

I am almost embarrassed to relate this story because my son Nate's faith totally outshone mine. My oldest son, Garrett, was college-bound, something we knew for years. My second son knew he needed to get training that would lead to a career where he could work with his hands, so probably not a four-year college. Together we explored options and went through career lists. Somehow, we had come across the occupation of a powerline technician, and it seemed to fit. Nate could be outside, work with his hands, and his dad was especially happy that linemen have good salaries. Nate and I drove out to a technical college not far away and met with the advisor. He applied, and we thought through communications sent to Nate that he was accepted into the linemen program. We rented an apartment in the area. We sat through a day-long orientation. At the end of the orientation, when it was time to sign up for classes, the advisor said Nate could sign up for one class and reapply next year for acceptance to the actual program. It is not really important about how the mix-up occurred; what is noteworthy is I lost my peace and even became angry. I am typically pretty mild-mannered. I am embarrassed to tell you how I missed God in this. After struggling for more than a week, I came across this prayer written under Nate's tab in my prayer journal. I had copied it from *The Power of a Praying Mom* by Stormie Omartian. The prayer is titled "Give My Child a Future of Peace." I will not include the whole prayer here, but here are some lines from it.

Lord, I pray for Nate to have a future that is
good, long, prosperous and secure because it is
in Your hands. Thank you that Your plans for
him are to bring peace and hope and a productive future. Turn Nate's heart toward You so that
he always has Your will and Your ways in mind.
Keep him from wasting time on a pathway you
will not bless.

I had in fact underlined *"keep him from wasting time on a pathway you will not bless."* Needless to say, God had this. Nate ended up going to a local school that has an urban forestry degree, and he is loving it. No, he may not make as much money, but being in God's will is always better. Nate's faith shone through as he dealt with this situation. He was the one who had to remind me that God was in control. It was me who had to learn a lesson in trust, and yes, I did write this down as a remembrance stone in my journal.

God has our kids and He does answer prayer and even when it takes us a minute (or a week) to recognize it!

Woman to love

I pray for their future spouses if that is the road God has for them. I pray God would work on that spouse's heart even now to bring them to a knowledge and understanding of God. However, not just that they would meet a godly spouse but that they would *be a godly spouse*—men who lead, love, and honor the opposite sex. Even if marriage is not in their future, there is a way men should respect and treat all women in their lives.

There is not a better prayer for husbands than the one found in Ephesians 5:25–31 (NIV):

> Husbands, love your wives, just as Christ loved the church and gave himself up for her to make her holy, cleansing her by the washing with water through the word, and to present her to himself as a radiant church, without stain or wrinkle or any other blemish, but holy and blameless. In this same way, husbands ought to love their wives as their own bodies. He who loves his wife loves himself. After all, no one ever hated their own body, but they feed and care for their body, just as Christ does the church—for we are members of his body. "For this reason a man will leave his

father and mother and be united to his wife, and
the two will become one flesh."

Our sons will leave us and make their own lives as God has said they should do, but we will always send them with our prayers.

Prayers for our Daughter's Future

As I was reviewing the prayers for my sons, I realized I had not been praying future prayers for my daughter or at least I did not have the same framework as I had taken from the *Knight* book. For the first few years with us, her trauma was often so evident and forefront that praying for the day was enough. However, we had been in a good routine for a while now, and I was convicted while writing this. As I was thinking about this and what that framework would look like for daughters, I happened to be reading through Acts in my morning prayer time. Acts 16 tells us about Lydia.

> On the Sabbath, we left the city and went down along the river where we had heard there was to be a prayer meeting. We took our place with the women who had gathered there and talked with them. One woman, Lydia, was from Thyatira and a dealer in expensive textiles, known to be a God—fearing woman. As she listened with intensity to what was being said, the Master gave her a trusting heart —and she believed! After she was baptized, along with everyone in her household, she said in a surge of hospitality, "If you're confident that I'm in this with you and believe in the Master truly, come home and be my guests." We hesitated, but she wouldn't take no for an answer.
> Acts 16:13–15 MSG

Much of what is written about Lydia here reminds me of the excellent wife described in Proverbs 31 (NASB). So we have two representations here: a single woman (Lydia may have always been single or was a widow) and a married woman, both of who are godly role models. This is the framework I gleaned from these two passages and the overlaps I drew. For our daughters' future and code of conduct, I pray that they are clothed *in* strength and dignity as displayed in these "ins."

- *Independent and industrious.* Lydia's independence is seen in her ability to use her skills as a businesswoman to run a successful textile business. In Proverbs 31, we see parallels as the wife considering a field and buying it, and from her earnings planting a vineyard (verse 16). Verse 13 reads, "She looks for wool and linen, And works with her hands in delight."

  May ____________ find where her individual strengths lie and develop those strengths to further the kingdom. May she take delight in her abilities and her work.

- *Intimate* relationship with God. Lydia was independent but she was also God dependent. Where do we first meet Lydia? At a prayer meeting. She was known to be a "God-fearing woman," and it states the "Master gave her a trusting heart." Lydia was actually the first European convert. In Proverbs 31, we read, "But a woman who fears the Lord, she shall be praised" (30b). We also read that she "smiles at the future" (25b). From this, we can observe that she trusts God with her future.

  May _________ as she grows learn to become dependent on her heavenly Father. Give her a trusting heart, a peace about the future.

- *Intrinsic* worth. Proverbs 31:30 states, "Charm is deceitful and beauty is vain, But a woman who fears the Lord, she shall be praised." She knows her internal worth. She is also true to herself taking care of her own needs. Verse 22 says, "She makes coverings for herself; Her clothing is fine linen and purple." Verse 18 says, "She senses that her profit is good" and the NIV states it as, "she senses the worth of her work."

May _____________ know her worth is in being Your daughter, not how she looks or what others think of her. May she treat herself as Your temple, taking care of her body, soul, and spirit. May she value her unique contribution to the world around her.

- *Influence* those around her for good. We see this exhibited in Lydia in verse 15: "After she was baptized, along with everyone in her household." We also see she used her position and home to serve Paul and Silas by welcoming them as guests in her home. In Proverbs 31, we see it in verses 11–12, "The heart of her husband trusts in her, And he will have no lack of gain. She does him good and not evil, All the days of her life." We also read she influences those outside of her family. In verse 20, it says, "She extends her hand to the poor, And she stretches out her hands to the needy." She also uses her wisdom and kindness to bless those around her (verse 26).

  May _____________ use her influence for the benefit of those in her immediate circle as well as reach out to others. May she display You in her daily life. May she impart kindness and wisdom to those around her.

- *Integrity* of character. We see Lydia's integrity must have been shown through to Paul and Silas. In their first visit, she implores them to come, but later on in Acts 16:40, we read that after Paul and Silas are released from prison, they go straight to Lydia's house. Comparably in Proverbs 31, we have read, "The heart of her husband trusts in her." Interestingly, one of the definitions of integrity in *Merriam-Webster* is "the quality or state of being complete or undivided." When we are committed to God, we are "complete" and "undivided."

  May _____________ demonstrate integrity in all she does, in work, in relationships. May she have an undivided heart and find her completeness in You.

I now include the whole prayer below so you can adapt it and pray for your daughter's future.

> May ___________ find where her individual strengths lie and develop those strengths to further the kingdom. May she take delight in her abilities and her work.
>
> May _________, as she grows, learn to become dependent on her heavenly Father. Give her a trusting heart, a peace about the future.
>
> May _____________ know her worth is in being Your daughter, not how she looks or what others think of her. May she treat herself as Your temple, taking care of her body, soul, and spirit. May she value her unique contribution to the world around her.
>
> May ___________ use her influence for the benefit of those in her immediate circle as well as reach out to others. May she display You in her daily life. May she impart kindness and wisdom to those around her.
>
> May _____________ demonstrate integrity in all she does, in work, in relationships. May she have an undivided heart and find her completeness in You and You alone.

Applications
Chapter 7: Prayer: Your Most Powerful Tool

1. What scripture prayers resonate with you for your children? List each child's name and write some individual prayers for them.

2. How are sibling relationships? (See the recommendations for the book *Close Kids*.) What areas need prayer?

3. Are you praying for good friends for each of your children?

4. What prayers are you praying for their child's future?

Conclusion

Final Words of Hope

Then I will give her her vineyards from there,
And the Valley of Achor as a door of hope.
Hosea 2:15 NASB

The Valley of Achor in the above verse actually means valley of trouble. Achor is actually the location Achan was stoned after disobeying God by taking valuables from their enemies when God commanded they should be destroyed. See Joshua 7. Yet through the valley of trouble, there is a door of hope. God produces hope in spite of circumstances. God uses us not because of our abilities but because we willingly lay down our lives before Him. We willingly take His hand and let Him lead us on our life journey.

Let me give you a very brief synopsis of my early years of life. I do this to show you that God uses us with all our flaws and imperfections. In our weakness, He is strong. I was an anxious, shy child. I am often not even sure why. My mom felt a need to defend me as a young child because others assumed I could not talk. I did talk, but only when I was comfortable and happy at home with my family. When in public, though, I hid behind my mom and sister whenever anyone addressed me. When I went to elementary school, I truly disliked being away from home. I would have been a great homeschool kid! Whenever I was called on in school, my face would grow hot and flushed, and the other students would notice. Nevertheless, God

131

instilled in me a strong sense of justice and with courage to look out for those who may not be able to speak up for themselves. I was well liked and often stood up for those less advantaged. Other kids did listen to me because I was genuinely kind to everyone. I think I may have started to blossom in middle school, but my dad went through a crisis and was eventually diagnosed bipolar. My dad came from a very dysfunctional home, and it is a miracle and absolutely to his credit that he has been able to overcome much of it. However, his mental illness took a toll on our family life.

It was a very difficult time because we could not explain his behaviors, and he did not receive a diagnosis for years. His behaviors made me want to hide once again, and I dealt with that all through high school. My senior year, I began dating a man from church who was a few years older than me. He was probably on the verge of being verbally abusive, yet I stayed with him almost all through college. This did nothing for my self-esteem. I still believe one of my best life decisions was to end that relationship for good. I thank God I did have a stubborn streak and was determined in many ways. Putting myself through college, I was determined to graduate in four years. I immediately got a job teaching, but I continued to struggle with anxiety, self-esteem, and feeling worthy. Although I may not have recognized it at that time, anxiety may have also driven the need to control my life choices. However, God used all my life circumstances to learn to trust Him and become more of who He created me to be. As you place your hand in God's hand, you, too, will use His strength to become your God created self.

Living in God's Strength

I would have not chosen my divorce, but it is how God showed me how much He loved me. He used me in all my weakness and in all His strength to raise two confident sons. Although still not easy for me, God has given me confidence to step out of my box time and time again to do work for Him. Psalm 84:5–6 (NIV) says, "Blessed are those whose strength is in you, whose hearts are set on pilgrimage. As they pass through the Valley of Baka, they make it a place of springs; the autumn rains also cover it with pools. They go from strength to strength, till each appears before God in Zion."

I will quote the *Moody Bible Commentary* to further explain this scripture.

> Passing through the valley of Baca ("weeping," v.6), the saddest of times, those who trust in the Lord can transform those tears and make the valley of weeping into a spring of water. People such as this go from strength to strength (v7a). No matter where they go or what their circumstances may be, God's strength is always available to them; and to "recharge" this strength they appear regularly before God in Zion.

On our pilgrimage, our life journey, we need to appear regularly before God because

> [h]e will not grow tired or weary, and his understanding no one can fathom. He gives strength to the weary, and increases the power of the weak. Even youths grow tired and weary, and young men stumble and fall; but those who hope in the LORD will renew their strength. They will soar on wings like eagles; they will run and not grow weary, they will walk and not be faint. Isaiah 40:28b–31 NIV

So, dear friend, you may not feel equipped for this journey, but with God leading, you are. It will not be easy, but you will grow exactly where you need to. I close with the ending words from Psalm 31:23–24 (MSG), which is the Psalm I opened with.

> Love the Lord, all his faithful people!
> The Lord preserves those who are true to him,
> but the proud he pays back in full.

Be strong and take heart,
all you who hope in the Lord.

Applications
Conclusion: Final Words of Hope

1. Reflect on your life story.

2. What is God teaching you on this journey?

3. In what areas are you growing?

4. In what areas do you need God's supernatural strength?

Acknowledgments

I thank God for being my guide and for fitting this book together. I thank my husband for having the grace to allow me write about parts of my life that are foreign to him. This is a hard thing when two people with pasts join together. I thank my parents for leading me into faith in Christ. I thank my sons for allowing me to write about vulnerable things in our lives and my daughter for her patience as I spent time writing.

CONNECT

Dear friend,

Please visit my website aimeecooks.com to connect with me. Here you will find free resources such as printables on changing your belief system, a collection of verses on forgiveness, and more.

May God be with you and give you strength for your journey,
Aimee Claire Cooks

Appendix

Sleep recommendations from the *Journal of Clinical Sleep Medicine* (published on June 15, 2016, https://doi.org/10.5664/jcsm.5866):

- Infants* 4 months to 12 months should sleep 12 to 16 hours per 24 hours (including naps) on a regular basis to promote optimal health.
- Children 1 to 2 years of age should sleep 11 to 14 hours per 24 hours (including naps) on a regular basis to promote optimal health.
- Children 3 to 5 years of age should sleep 10 to 13 hours per 24 hours (including naps) on a regular basis to promote optimal health.
- Children 6 to 12 years of age should sleep 9 to 12 hours per 24 hours on a regular basis to promote optimal health.
- Teenagers 13 to 18 years of age should sleep 8 to 10 hours per 24 hours on a regular basis to promote optimal health.
- Recommendations for infants younger than 4 months are not included due to the wide range of normal variation in duration and patterns of sleep and insufficient evidence for associations with health outcomes.

REFERENCES

Chapter 1: Know Your Guide

Ahrons, Constance. 1994. *The Good Divorce*. New York, HarperPerennial (referred to this book, but not recommended reading).

Brown, Sharon Garlough. 2013. *Sensible Shoes*. Downers Grove, IL: IVP Books.

2022. "Grief." Vocabulary.com Inc., a division of IXL Learning, https://www.vocabulary.com/dictionary/grief.

Rydelnik, Michael, and Michael Vanlaningham. 2014. *Moody Bible Commentary*. Chicago: Moody Publishers.

2000. *The American Heritage Dictionary of the English Language, Fourth Edition*. Boston: Houghton Mifflin Company.

1985. *The NIV Study Bible*. Grand Rapids: Zondervan Bible Publishers.

Chapter 2: Trust Your Guide

Bonhoeffer, Dietrich. 1978. *Life Together*. New York: HarperOne.

Elhridge, John. 2016. *Moving Mountains: Praying with Passion, Confidence, and Authority*. Thomas Nelson.

Mears, Henrietta C. 2002. *What the Bible Is All About: Bible Handbook*. Venture, CA: Regal Books.

2023. "Moved." Merriam-Webster, Incorporated, https://www.merriam-webster.com/dictionary/move.

Peterson, Eugene. 2007. *Conversations: The Message with Its Translator*. Colorado Springs: NavPress.

Peterson, Eugene. 2021. *On Living Well*. Colorado Springs: Waterbrook.

1985. *The NIV Study Bible*. Grand Rapids: Zondervan Bible Publishers.

Chapter 3: Hidden Traps

Cloud, Dr. Henry, and Dr. John Townsend. 1992. *Boundaries*. Grand Rapids: Zondervan.

Deal, Ron. 2014. *The Smart Stepfamily: Seven Steps to a Healthy Family*. Grand Rapids: Bethany House Publishers.

2023. "Intimate." Merriam-Webster, Incorporated, https://www.merriam-webster.com/dictionary/intimate.

Marquardt, Elizabeth. 2005. *Between Two Worlds: The Inner Lives of Children of Divorce*. New York: Three Rivers Press.

Lucado, Max. 2017. *Anxious for Nothing: Finding Calm in a Chaotic World*. Nashville: Thomas Nelson.

Ortlund, Dane. 2020. *Gentle and Lowly: The Heart of Christ for Sinners and Sufferers*. Wheaton, IL: Crossway.

Rydelnik, Michael, and Michael Vanlaningham. 2014. *Moody Bible Commentary*. Chicago: Moody Publishers.

Rydelnik, Michael, and Michael Vanlaningham. 2014. *Moody Bible Commentary*. Chicago: Moody Publishers.

1985. *The NIV Study Bible*. Grand Rapids: Zondervan Bible Publishers.

Chapter 4: Your Children

Marquardt, Elizabeth. 2005. *Between Two Worlds: The Inner Lives of Children of Divorce*. New York: Three Rivers Press.

Music, Bethel, Jonathan David Helser, Melissa Helser. "No Longer Slaves." Bethel Music. https://bethelmusic.com/resources/peace/no-longer-slaves.

Tripp, Paul. August 21, 2017. *"Don't Forget about the Boy,"* Paul Tripp Ministries Inc. https://www.paultripp.com/articles/posts/dont-forget-about-the-boy.

Chapter 5: Single Parenting

Dobson, Dr. James. 1978. *The Strong Willed Child.* Wheaton: Tyndale House.

Jones, Stan, and Brenna. 2019. *God's Design for Sex Series—Revised and Updated Edition.* Colorado Springs: NavPress.

Lewis, Robert. 2007. *Raising a Modern-Day Knight: A Father's Role in Guiding His Son to Authentic Manhood.* Carol Stream, IL: Tyndale House Publishers.

Marquardt, Elizabeth. 2005. *Between Two Worlds: The Inner Lives of Children of Divorce.* New York: Three Rivers Press.

Moffit, Terrie, Richie Poulton, and Avshalom Caspi. September/October 2013. "Lifelong Impact of Early Self-Control" 2023 Sigma Xi, The Scientific Research Honor Society. https://www.americanscientist.org/article/lifelong-impact-of-early-self-control.

Olson Laney, Marti. 2005. *The Hidden Gift of the Introverted Child: Helping Your Child Thrive in an Extroverted World.* New York: Workman Publishing.

Paruthi, Shalini et. al. 2016. "Recommended Amount of Sleep for Pediatric Populations: A Consensus Statement of the American Academy of Sleep Medicine." *Journal of Clinical Sleep Medicine*, 12, no. 6. https://aasm.org/resources/pdf/pediatricsleepdurationconsensus.pdf.

Weinberger, Jesse. 2014. *The Boogeyman Exists and He's in Your Child's Back Pocket.* Coppell, TX: Create Space Independent Publishing Platform.

Chapter 6: Rebuilding Your Family

Mears, Dr. Henrietta C. 1984. *What the Bible Is All About: Bible Handbook NIV Edition*. Ventura, CA: Regal.

Rydelnik, Michael, and Michael Vanlaningham. 2014. *Moody Bible Commentary*. Chicago: Moody Publishers.

Chapter 7: Prayer: Your Most Powerful Tool

Lewis, Robert. 2007. *Raising a Modern-Day Knight: A Father's Role in Guiding His Son to Authentic Manhood*. Carol Stream, IL: Tyndale House Publishers.

Nichols, Fern. 2003. *Every Child Needs a Praying Mom*. Grand Rapids: Zondervan.

Omartian, Stormie. 2015. *The Power of a Praying Mom: Powerful Prayers for You and Your Children*. Eugene, Oregon: Harvest House.

Peterson, Eugene. 2007. *Conversations: The Message with Its Translator*. Colorado Springs: NavPress.

Final Words of Hope

Rydelnik, Michael, and Michael Vanlaningham. 2014. *Moody Bible Commentary*. Chicago: Moody Publishers.

Recommended Reading and Resources

The public library is a great resource for books. I often check out books I am interested in to determine if it is a book I desire to invest money into. Books I find myself wanting to underline are ones that make my purchase list!

For Personal Bible Study and Prayer

- *What the Bible Is All About: Bible Handbook NIV Edition*—Dr. Henrietta C. Mears
- *A Journey to Victorious Praying: Finding Discipline and Delight in Your Prayer Life*—Bill Thrasher
- *Moving Mountains: Praying with Passion, Confidence, and Authority*—John Eldredge
- *The Power of a Praying Parent: Book of Prayers*—Stormie Omartian

For Personal and Spiritual Growth

- *Boundaries*—Dr. Henry Cloud and Dr. John Townsend
- *Boundaries for Your Soul: How to Turn our Overwhelming Thoughts and Feelings into Your Greatest Allies*—Alison Cook and Kimberly Miller
- *Healing Is a Choice: Ten Decisions That Will Transform Your Life & Ten Lies That Can Prevent You from Making Them*—Steve Aterbun

I really appreciate this book. Although it is not specifically about divorce, Steve shares components of his life and how he processed his divorce.

- *Gentle and Lowly: The Heart of Christ for Sinners and Sufferers*—Dane Ortlund
- *When the Bottom Drops Out: Finding Grace in the Depths of Disappointment*—Robert Bugh
- *Choosing Forgiveness: Your Journey to Freedom*—Nancy Leigh DeMoss

For Parents of Children of Any Age

- *Between Two Worlds: The Inner Lives of Children of Divorce*—Elizabeth Marquardt
- *Gist: The Essence of Raising Life Ready Kids*—Michael W. Anderson and Timothy D. Johanson

  One of my all-time favorite parenting books. I have picked it up and reread it many times and found it applicable to all age stages.
- *The Hidden Gifts of the Introverted Child*—Marti Olsen Laney
- *Close Kids: Connect Your Children for Life*—Brett A. Johnston
- Any parenting book by Dr. Kevin Leman (his humor makes his books even fun to read!)

For Listening

- *Focus on the Family Broadcast* (https://www.focusonthefamily.com/shows/broadcast/)
- *Family Life* (https://www.familylife.com/how-to-listen-to-familylifes-podcasts/)

For Moms

- *That's My Son: How Moms Can Influence Boys to Become Men of Character*—Rick Johnson
- *Every Child Needs a Praying Mom*—Fern Nichols
- *The Power of a Praying Mom: Powerful Prayers for You and Your Children*—Stormie Omartian

For Dads

- *Better Dads, Stronger Sons: How Fathers Can Guide Boys to Become Men of Character*—Rick Johnson
- *Raising a Modern-Day Knight: A Father's Role in Guiding His Son to Authentic Manhood*—Robert Lewis

For Sons

- *Bringing Up Boys*—Dr. James Dobson
- *Created for Work: Practical Insights for Young Men*—Bob Schultz

For Daughters

- *Praying for Girls: Asking God for the Things They Need Most*—Teri Lynne Underwood

For Teens

- *The 5 Love Languages of Teenagers*—Gary Chapman
- *Raising Teens in a Contrary Culture*—Mark Gregston

For Those Sensitive Topics

- *God Made All of Me: A Book to Help Children Protect Their Bodies*—Justin S. Holcomb and Lindsey A. Holcomb

- *Good Pictures, Bad Pictures: Porn-Proofing Today's Young Kids*—Kristen A. Jenson
- *God's Design for Sex Series—Revised and Updated Edition*—Stan and Brenna Jones
- *The Ultimate Puberty Book for Girls: Celebrate Your Body*—Sonya Renee Taylor

Fair warning: This is not a Christian book; I did have to tear out two pages. However, it was a very comprehensive book. It was well-written and covered everything from body changes to friends and peer pressure. I would be cautious if you buy an updated version. Look it over first.

Feeling Wheel Links

- https://www.imom.com/printables/ (There is a feeling wheel simplified for younger children under the behavior tab.)
- https://theparentcue.org/ (Under the "Resources" tab and there is also guidance on how to use it with teens.)

About the Author

Aimee Claire Cooks was a divorced single mom raising two young sons for many years. Navigating through rebuilding their family unit after the divorce and parenting through a high-conflict situation has given her a unique understanding of the repercussions of divorce on families. With a passion for children and godly parenting, Aimee desires for you to grow into a more intimate relationship with Jesus as you navigate your unique circumstances and provide leadership for your family.

She has a bachelor of science degree in early childhood education with a dual certification in both special and regular education. Combining her educational background with biblical principles, God gave her needed wisdom in parenting divorced. She is proud of her sons and so grateful to God that they are launching into adulthood as healthy individuals despite circumstances.

Aimee taught for twenty-four years in various settings before God directed her down a new path, homeschooling her adopted daughter. She has been remarried to her husband Ryan for ten years adding two stepchildren. She and Ryan fostered and adopted their daughter five years ago. They live in Wisconsin and cherish spending time with their family, preferably outdoors!